R A W   F A I T H

For F. B.

And in a special way for Isaac T., who taught me
many things,
but especially never to look back.

With special gratitude to Robert Hamma, who
brought to
this book rare insight, sympathy, and skill.

To Frank Cunningham, who continues to bring his
great
building skills to the service of a vision.

And to a supportive friend, Patrick McGeary, who can
always be depended on to get the word out.

John Kirvan

Author of God Hunger

RAW FAITH

NURTURING THE BELIEVER IN ALL OF US

SORIN BOOKS
Notre Dame, Indiana

John Kirvan is the author of *God Hunger: Discovering the Mystic in All of Us*, a companion volume to this work, and of the highly successful *Thirty Days with a Great Spiritual Teacher* series, a library of fourteen books which offer the wisdom of the mystics for daily meditation. He currently lives in Southern California where he writes primarily about classical spirituality.

International Standard Book Number: 1-893732-18-5

Library of Congress Catalog Card Number: 00-101262

Cover design by Angela Moody, *Moving Images.*

Text design by Katherine Robinson Coleman and Amy Crownover.

Printed and bound in the United States of America.

CONTENTS

From the author-

I have known since I was very young that every time I confessed my belief in God I have had to add, "help thou my unbelief." I know that in this I am not alone.

Along the way I have come to accept that our spiritual journey will not be a way of easy certitude and satisfaction, but a way of unfathomable mystery, faith, and contradictions. It will be a life lived with a God who in the end remains unknown and unknowable, a life with the world's expectations turned upside down. The journey is called "apophatic"—a time honored way of approaching God that stretches from the insights of Gregory of Nyssa in the fourth century, through *The Cloud of Unknowing* in the fourteenth, to Simone Weil in the twentieth century.

Raw Faith and its companion book, *God Hunger,* are at their roots prayerful journals of an unquenchable hunger for God, a journey that can be nourished only in faith and lived out in hope. For me, it has been and remains a journey taken in the dependable company of the great Christian, Jewish, and Islamic mystics who have traveled this way before, whose insights have enlightened the journey and inspired these books.

I wish you well on your journey.

John Kirvan

PART ONE

Believing

The "believer" of the future will be a mystic or he or she will not exist at all—if by mysticism we mean, not singular parapsychological phenomena, but a genuine experience of God emerging from the very heart of our existence.

..

The spirituality of the future will not be supported or at any rate will be much less supported by a sociologically homogeneity of its situation; it will have to live much more clearly than hitherto out of a solitary immediate experience of God and his spirit in the individual.

In such a situation the lonely responsibility of the individual in his or her decision of faith is necessary and required in a way much more radical than it was in former times.

—KARL RAHNER

Faith begins with a voice out of the dark that speaks to a hunger so deep that nothing but God can satisfy it. And nothing but raw faith can respond to it and sustain it.

**

I was nineteen, a novice seeking entry into a religious community. If truth be told I was more bored than spiritually anguished when I walked through the snow that winter night for the spiritual direction I was expected to seek out. I went to talk with a simple—we thought him not too bright— kind and holy man. It was something you should do, something expected of an earnest young seeker. I presumed that most of my companions had already made the journey, maybe all of them. He might think there was something spiritually lacking in me if I didn't follow their lead. More likely than not, however, I went to see him just to have someone to talk with, someone with whom to break the quiet and solitude of a winter night. I was probably also looking for some way to inject a little drama into excruciatingly routine days. Concocting and parading an agonized soul was as good a way as any. I can't remember what question, what agony I settled on to justify my visit and convince him of my sincerity. But I do remember his response.

After listening to my manufactured troubles he said:

"Don't you believe in God?"

I felt in that instant—as I have so often since—that I was an impostor who had been found out. I didn't know the answer to his question. He had obviously seen through my pieties and my posturing to reveal the empty soul of someone who might know all the words of faith and all its gestures— all the ways to elicit the wise words of a spiritual director— but who in that moment could not say for sure whether or not he believed.

Only later did I understand that his question was rhetorical. He meant only to reassure me that my worries were groundless, that I simply lacked confidence in God's amazing grace, that I should relax, trust my Father, that all was and would be well. But what I heard was something else altogether.

**

I knew in that moment that I was not being asked whether or not I thought that God existed.

I was being asked whether or not I believed in God.

This is not at all the same question.

You can answer the first in a thousand faith-escaping ways. You can answer "yes" to the second only by risking your life. And that was what I instantly understood on that winter night.

God could never be an escape from the storm.

I have never recovered from that shattering moment. Nor for all its unsettling of my heart, all its dislodging of my securities, do I want to. I am content to have the question so resident in my soul that hardly a day can go by without my hearing it.

"Don't you believe in God?"

Having heard that question repeated in my soul over and over again I have never once been able to say, "I believe," without in the same breath convicting myself of arrogance, without pleading for help in my unbelief.

I have never since been able to convince myself that church membership, liturgy, sacraments, prayers regularly said, meditations made, spiritual books consumed, young dreams of holiness, the turbulence and satisfactions of middle years, and above all, creeds assented to—that any of these, that all of these together can add up to belief in God.

I have, in fact, come to feel that my church membership has let me off the hook, allowing me to substitute an acknowledged and accepted creed for belief. It has let me off far too easily.

Faith, I know now, is not a simple profession of what you accept as true . . . not something stirred up in moments of grandeur or terror. . . . Not a spiritual grace note to an ordinary life. . . . Not spiritual brand loyalty.

Faith is something else again.

It is at once another way of knowing what is most familiar to us and at the same time coming to know a world beyond the familiar, beyond everything that can be reached by our mind and senses.

It is what you do, how you respond in the face of the unfathomable mystery that lies at the core of everything we are, of everything we experience.

Faith is about an unknowable God and about ourselves at that point where we become a mystery, and the mystery of God becomes personal. Not the God or self that is summarized in a chapter of the catechism for easy commitment to memory. Not a God or self that is squeezed into our own image and likeness and circumscribed by our faltering words, but the God and self that is by definition indefinable.

Faith is about what is uncapturable and radically unknowable, a mystery that cannot be approached in any other way than by surrender, by letting go of our securities.

Faith is our submission to, our embrace of the unknowable as the cornerstone of our lives.

Belief, as Kathleen Norris has reminded us, is a word that has Greek roots, where it means: "to give one's heart to."

There is something raw, open, unfinished about such faith.

To truly believe is to turn our lives upside down. It is to shatter our expectations and our certainties. It is to color, ground, define, in a fundamentally different way, how we relate not just to God but to ourselves, our neighbors, and the world in which we live.

It is to see all that is and can be in a different light.

It is to live convinced that what matters, what is most real cannot be seen or measured, and that from beyond and beneath the surface of our lives there comes a question that demands a response, a voice that deserves the full attention of our hunger-shaped soul.

"Don't you believe in me?"

When a *Los Angeles Times* writer told Denzel Washington that God was "hip" now, the actor straightened him out. "To say God is hip, that's the ego trying to bring him down to our level of understanding. We can't even understand why we woke up, but we got to put God where we can understand him. Man goes down to the ocean and tries to fit the knowledge of the ocean into his brain, instead of just jumping in the water."

God-centered faith requires our "jumping in the water." It requires our transformation. No wonder most of us would prefer dipping our toes to taking our chances and transforming our lives. Many of us would prefer never to take that leap. All of us at some time or another would prefer the comfort of a spirituality that does not require faith, preferring a less demanding, manageable, comprehensible God. I plead guilty. I have never learned to swim. To be over my head terrifies me. I am an authority on toe dipping. I know nothing about plunging.

I have been tempted, often content, to put my faith in a thousand different stand-ins for God who did not require me to unsettle my ways.

They are readily available.

I think of the best-selling author of a multi-book series who promised in an interview that his new book—in which God will continue to talk with him—will continue his mission of taking the mystery out of God—cutting him down to size, our size, fitting him into our brain, bringing him "down to our level of understanding." After all, an understandable God does not require us to uproot our lives. A mystery-free God would be very "cool" indeed, perfect for an age when to be spiritual is to be cool and uncommitted.

But it has always been thus.

At every turn of the path, hucksters of the spirit have met every generation in search of food for their God-hungry souls, fast-food merchants who hold out the promise that faith is not necessary.

God-look-a-likes will do—anything, anyone that can end-run the need for faith by making it unnecessary. Most of the time, however, we need not look outside ourselves, because deep in our souls we harbor the suspicion that we are God, that the only God we need is one created in our own image and likeness.

But for a God-hungry soul this is a starvation diet. And our soul lets us know it with hunger pangs that won't go away.

There is no substitute for God.

There is no substitute for mystery encountered.
As a result there is no substitute for faith.

**

At its most basic and most profound, at its rawest, faith means letting go of everything that most of us have come to depend on for the meaning and security of our lives, letting go of security itself.

The centuries have used two symbols for this "letting go." We have called it a leap. And we have called it walking on water. In both images we are called upon to leave behind us the solid footing of the world we have always known.

Our leap is into the unknown and the unknowable. There is nothing but air at our feet, and in our ear the voice that repeats: "Let go. Trust me. I am here. Everything you hunger for is waiting for you." And so we leap, or freeze at the edge of the abyss, or poise a hundred times, one foot in the air, until one day the voice is irresistible, the risk acceptable.

Or we hear the voice in the dark of the night. Often when the waves are heaviest, the currents most treacherous, he appears, walking on water. It is a ghost, we think, a fantasy, an illusion, anything but reality. Our soul cries out in fear, but immediately he speaks to us: "Take heart. It is I. Have no fear."

In the Christian tradition there is Peter's story. He answered such a voice on such a night. "Lord, if it is you," he said, "let me come to you on the water." Jesus said: "Come." So Peter got out of the boat and walked on water and approached Jesus; but when he felt the wind, he was afraid, and beginning to sink he cried out: "Lord save me." Jesus immediately reached out his hand and caught him, saying to him, "O you of little faith, why did you doubt?" (Mt 14:28 ff.).

Centuries later, in the short story "Wise Blood," Flannery O'Connor would tell the story of Hazel Moates. In the back of his mind Hazel would see "a wild ragged figure motioning him to turn around and come off into the dark where he was not sure of his footing, where he might be walking on water and not know it and then suddenly know it and drown."

"Don't you believe in me?"

I have learned over the years—as so many of us have—to blunt the question, to blanch faith's rawness, to smooth its cutting edges and to polish it into respectability. I have learned to anaesthetize my soul against its sharpness and demands so that I hardly know any longer what raw faith is, and what truly it is to live at the edge of nothingness in a cloud of unknowing. I have learned to fend off its peace, to distrust its joy.

But the question does not go away. The invitation is not retracted. The opportunity is not forever lost.

**

You and I are not the first persons to stand at the edge, gathering our courage to leap. We are not the first to take halting steps on stormy water. Nor are we the first to be afraid of the dark. There are the millions from every generation, culture, and spiritual tradition who have responded to the same invitation that we have heard from out of the dark, from beneath and beyond the surface of the world we share.

They are the "believers" who have made the leap, who have walked on water, who have chosen life in the dark, who have made raw faith the cornerstone of their spiritual lives. They are the believers who invite us to join them. They promise to be at our side. For the abyss does not disappear. The waters do not become calm. The wound does not heal. The dark does not evaporate.

In the pages that follow you will find ten such companions matched with themes of faith that inspired and supported them. None of them exhausted the experience of God. Each of them in their own way and words opened a small window on the mystery that so captivates us. Each of them in their own words described what they saw through a small opening into the dark. Each of them is anxious to share with us.

We need only to reach out and take their hands.

Beyond and beneath the lives and words of these companions is another more personal story. You will find here the prayer journal of one seeker, the writer of these pages. I cannot promise anything else. In the long run it is the only story I know. It is a tale of clinging to belief on a journey made with those who said it could be done, who have kept alive for me the question from that winter night so long ago.

"Don't you believe in me?"

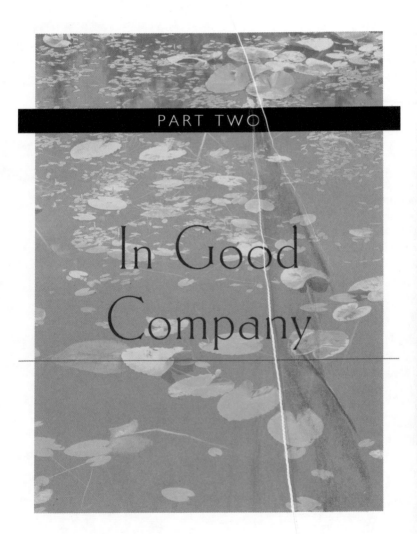

PART TWO

In Good Company

Whoever multiplies words causes confusion.
The Truth that can be spoken
is not the Ultimate Truth.
Ultimate Truth is wordless,
the silence within the silence.
More than the absence of speech,
more than the absence of words,
Ultimate Truth is the seamless being-in-place
that comes with attending to Reality.

—SHIMON BEN GAMLIEL

In the end searching for God is not a journey of the mind but of the soul. Ideas surrender to wonder. Words are a pathway into silence. And light ends in the darkness of a God who escapes our every effort at definition.

Raw Faith, therefore, is not a series of scholarly essays meant for study, but meditations meant for praying, for unwrapping the mystery, pulling back one veil at a time, knowing with each hope-filled, tentative gesture that the veils are without number, the mystery beyond plumbing.

In these pages, prompted by the lives and writings of ten of the great spiritual teachers, we are invited to explore ten basic elements of classical Western spirituality—ten faces of faith.

There is no special order to the themes that are reflected upon. You can approach them as you choose. They are so many arrows pointing at an indefinable center of mystery.

This exploration, however, if it is to lead anywhere, must be conducted with your heart open, from that place within you that Dag Hammarskjold calls "a center of stillness surrounded by silence." What we seek on our journey is not a solution to a problem, not the answer to a question, but an encounter with the mystery of faith that will by very definition far exceed the best efforts of our minds, the uttermost limits of our imaginations.

We are not asked to abandon our intelligence or surrender our sanity but to rely on the tools of the spirit, several of which are employed in the exploration of each theme.

Each section is introduced with an "epigram," a meditation-provoking passage taken from the writings of a great spiritual teacher. I ask you to do what I did. As I read the works of the great mystics a passage would leap out at me. On another day, perhaps it might have been another passage. No matter. I would stop and pray it through. In this book I invite you to do the same. And be aware that in prayer you never need be alone. Bring someone with you—one of the great mystics whose words and life have inspired this book. I have added a short reading that develops the epigram and introduces the life and times of the teacher, the world in which they experienced God, and the unique characteristics of their experience. What is important to understand is that these short passages are not meant to tell the whole story of their lives and sanctity, but just to create a doorway large enough to let us into their lives.

Then come five exercises for the soul, each designed to involve us in the three great classic prayer forms of western spirituality.

There are mantras: short, pithy, often epigrammatic sentences that by way of paradox and irony catch the essence of a great spiritual truth. They are easily committed to memory and often make their impact by constant repetition.

There are short spiritual readings—meditations. It is a form of prayer that best allows us to summon up silence, to focus our wildly work-family-news-distracted souls. These meditations, although prompted by the words of a mystic, are my own. They are not meant to summarize the insights of a great teacher. They are not a substitute for reading their words, for directly contemplating their experience of God. They are merely a record of how one person responded to something they said. You will have your own response. Trust it.

And finally there are short intercessionary prayers in which we speak directly to the God whose presence we celebrate. Some would say that this is the most revealing of all our prayers, for in this moment we speak to the God in whom we truly believe, the one we address—as someone has said—when nobody else is listening. You may use the words provided, but your own by definition will be more revealing, more searching. Note too that even though these prayers are cast as night prayers, you can pray them whenever you are looking for words to center your day.

How should you use these exercises? Any way you want. On any schedule, at any interval that is convenient, comfortable and/or rewarding. Do the meditation in the morning if you prefer, and the prayer at night. Or the whole thing in one snatched period of quiet. Do what you want. But do exercise an element of regularity. Without it you could miss out because of mere forgetfulness or laziness, or because you just don't feel like praying today.

But we must not forget as we explore the experience of those who have gone before, as we exercise our own souls in this pursuit of mystery, that our personal quest for a living faith is at its depth a unique moment in history. Millions have preceded us. But this is the first time we and God have met. There has never been anyone quite like us. There has never been a spiritual moment quite like this. One of the great theologians of this century, Karl Rahner, puts it this way: "Each individual man or woman is a unique and unrepeatable term of

God's creative love. Each must find their path to God in a way that is proper to themselves."

Be prepared to be surprised, because no one is more surprising than God. In the end we may, as the Kabbalah says, despite our most careful planning and the most demanding discipline, "stumble" onto God. "Whoever delves into mysticism cannot help but stumble, as it is written: 'This stumbling block is our hand. We cannot grasp these things unless we stumble over them.'"

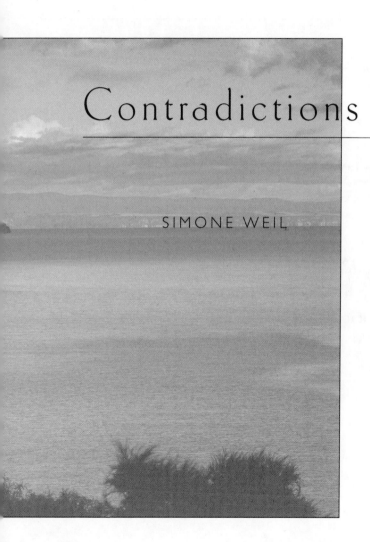

Contradictions

SIMONE WEIL

A case of contradictories, both of them true.
There is a God.
There is no God.
Where is the problem?
I am quite sure there is a God
in the sense that I am sure
my love is no illusion.
I am quite sure there is no God,
in the sense that I am sure
there is nothing
which resembles what I can conceive
when I say the word.

—SIMONE WEIL

Contradictions

It is a temptation to tame the most demanding contradictions of the spiritual life by turning them into platitudes. We may gentrify them into paradoxes, mere twists and turns of language; or declare the contradictions to be only apparent. More usually we simply eliminate one of the terms in order to erase the contradiction and our own unease.

It is to be a believer or to be an unbeliever.

But in Simone Weil we encounter someone for whom undiluted contradiction is the heart of the matter.

"There is a God. There is no God."

She is not playing a word game, not being clever or cute. She is cutting to the heart of faith. She is talking about holding contradictories together, not dissolving them. She rejects what is almost certainly our first response: "Something has to give. We can't have it both ways."

Weil insists not that we *can* have it both ways but that we *must* have it both ways. *"There is a God. There is no God."* For her faith is about holding the contradiction together. It is about not letting go of one or another side of the contradiction in order to ease our way, in order to make faith unnecessary.

What is critical is to understand that this embrace of contradiction is not a solution to an intellectual puzzle. Contradiction is the way in which we daily experience the world and life itself. It is an accurate description of the real world in which we live and therefore in which we meet and respond to God.

Our world is not tidy and the role of faith is not to tidy it up.

Our world is mysterious and the role of faith is not to dissolve the mysteries, but to find a way of exploring them, growing with them, growing into them. The response is not to eliminate the contradiction, but to understand, accept, and even desire them. A life of faith is one that suspends your life between truths that not only sound like a contradiction, but which are in fact contradictory.

"I am quite sure there is a God. . . . I am quite sure there is no God."

She is certain that her love is no illusion. She is equally sure that any God her words can capture does not exist.

Contradiction remains, therefore so does faith.

Simone Weil

(1909-1943)

For those who like their spirituality "neat," complete with a "good spirituality stamp of approval" Simone Weil (pronounced "vey") can be an uncomfortable companion. Her endorsements come from unexpected sources. Andre Gide called her the saint of all outsiders, T. S. Eliot and Albert Camus would join him in declaring her one of our century's foremost thinkers.

Not the usual endorsements for a saint.

But for those who can live with contradiction, she is a model of a "new sanctity" about which she wrote so provocatively and convincingly.

"Today," she wrote, "it is not nearly enough merely to be a saint, but we must have the saintliness demanded by the present moment, a new saintliness, itself also without precedent."

The Web site *If Monks Had Macs* for whom she is the patron philosopher summed up her own journey to a new sanctity this way:

> She wrote with the clarity of a brilliant mind educated in the best French schools, the social conscience of a grass-roots labor organizer, and the certainty and humility of a Christian mystic.
>
> Despite her rapturous love of Jesus Christ, she never ceased to study the truths of the religions of the East. She stayed outside of any church, but her passionate need to share the sufferings of others led her to fight with the anarchists in the Spanish Civil War, to work as a field hand and an unskilled laborer, and ultimately to die in England at the age of thirty-four from tuberculosis complicated by her refusing to eat more than Hitler's rations allotted to her countrymen in occupied France.

Saintliness has never been an abstraction. It has never been "something out there" that we adopt like clothing or memorize as though it were a formula to be employed. It will always be shaped not just by tested principles but by the demands of the given moment in which we live and to whose questions we must respond.

We make our act of faith here and now, in the only time and place available to us.

I

To believe in God is not a decision we can make. All we can do is decide not to give our love to false Gods.

—SIMONE WEIL

The textbook phrase "faith is a gift" has never been more deeply and simply understood that it was by Simone Weil.

We don't, she reminded us, qualify for faith. We don't achieve it or earn it or deserve it. We cannot decide to believe in the way that we decide to be a Presbyterian or a vegetarian. These sorts of things are up to us.

But faith is not up to us. Our believing in God is totally God's doing. The best we can do is to say "no" to the false Gods we meet along the way and consent to the offer God makes of himself. Believing in God is to see things as she sees them and only God can give us that sight.

It is a change of vision that is offered to everyone. It can be refused or go unrecognized or unappreciated but it cannot be taught, achieved, worked up to or engineered. What we can do is give our consent. "We are created for this consent, and for this alone."

For too many of us however, our life story is a tale of consent withheld.

LET US PRAY

As this night begins,
I know that the best I can hope for
is the humility not to say no
to your offer of faith.
Let me not,
out of cowardice,
or pride,
or the need to do it my way
withhold my consent to your love.
Let me do it your way.

2

My business is to think about God.
It is for God to think about me.

—SIMONE WEIL

Even in our most prayerful moments it is hard for us to surrender center stage. "Enough about me! Tell me, God: what do you think of me?"

Keeping your eyes on your self, "looking out" for your self, acting as though your life were in your hands—and your hands only—may have been passed on as self-preserving wisdom. But it gets life backward. It is the opposite of wisdom.

God will think about us. Trust him.

Our task is to think about God, which is to think about the unthinkable. But more fundamentally it is to stop thinking about ourselves by starting to think about God. It is to stop miring our soul in our own words, our own limited vision. It is to stop looking in the mirror. It is to stop talking about ourselves and calling it prayer. God is at ease with silence. It is we who are uncomfortable. He understands our silence, and is content with it, especially with the silence that happens when we approach him and are left speechless—the silence that happens when we try to think about God.

The silence that happens when we try to find words for him.

Our business is to think about God. God will do all the thinking about us that is necessary.

LET US PRAY

As this night begins,
let me fold my self
back into the shadows
so I can see more clearly what matters.
Let me be silent so you can speak,
so that I can hear.
Let me empty my hands
so I can take your hand
and trust in what you want for me.
You will think about me.
I trust you.

3

Looking is what saves us.

—SIMONE WEIL

For Simone Weil the spiritual journey is about looking, that is, it is about turning one's eyes towards God.

It is not about seeing God. Just looking.

It is about desire, not fulfillment, about hunger recognized, but not satisfied.

It is "waiting for God." It is not overtaking God.

What it is not, above all else, is "possession." It is Eve in the garden content to look and not to eat. It is exercising our freedom by turning our eyes to God or refusing to turn them.

Our turning or not turning—our looking—is the heart of our spiritual search because this is as much as we can do. It is as much as we need do.

We must be content to look from afar, and not convince ourselves that we have arrived.

We are just lookers.

LET US PRAY

As this night begins,
let me be content to wait for you
here in the darkness.
Let me turn my eyes to you and accept
that this is what I must do,
and all that I can do.
That I must be content to look
in your direction
and not see,
to reach out
without possessing you.
To know that turning my eyes to you
is what matters.

4

We cannot take a single step toward heaven.

—SIMONE WEIL

There's more "yellow brick road" and "emerald city" in our spirituality than we care to admit.

"Progress, getting somewhere, getting ahead" are activist, economic, political images stubbornly underlying our sense of spiritual fulfillment.

We have a feeling that if we walk straight ahead we will reach heaven. God, we presume, is at the end of a straight line, a level road. Everyday, in every way, we get closer and closer by putting one foot in front of the other.

But there is none of the above in the vision of Simone Weil.

God is not "ahead" of us. God is "above" us. God is the vertical dimension.

And vertical in her insight is precisely what is beyond our efforts. We have to be raised up, caught up by grace.

But the image implies more. It means letting go, it means surrendering, it means permitting ourselves to be taken up.

"It is not in our power to travel in a vertical direction. If, however we look heavenward for a long time, God comes and takes us up."

LET US PRAY

As this night begins,
let me look
where my eyes cannot take me
to see what I cannot see.
Let me surrender
so that I can go
where I am meant to be,
where I most want to be.
Let me
look heavenward.
Raise my eyes.
Raise my heart.

5

The hunger of the soul is not a belief,
it is a certainty.

—SIMONE WEIL

"The danger," Simone Weil wrote, "is not that the soul should doubt whether there is any bread [God], but that, by a lie, it should persuade itself that it is not hungry."

In the extraordinary introduction to her *Waiting for God*, the great America literary critic Leslie Fiedler put it this way: "Here below we must be content to be eternally hungry; indeed we must welcome hunger, for it is the sole proof we have of the reality of God who is the only sustenance that can satisfy us but one which is 'absent' in the created world."

A hunger like this could come from nowhere else, could be for nothing less.

And it cannot be a passing hunger. It must be an eternal state of soul.

How do I know there is a God?

Because I am hungry!

LET US PRAY

Let this night
begin in truth:
I am hungry
for what only you can give.
But more often than not
I have lied to myself.
I have denied my hunger,
settling for whatever
made no demands,
not bread but stones.
Let this night begin in truth.
I am hungry.
And you are there in my hunger.

Trust

HENRI J. M. NOUWEN

I can only fly freely
when I know there is a catcher to catch me.
If we are to take risks,
to be free,
in the air,
in life,
we have to know
that when we come down from it all,
we're going to be caught,
we're going to be safe.
The great hero is the least visible.
Trust the catcher.

—HENRI NOUWEN

Trust

A trapeze flyer and his catcher is the kind of brilliant spiritual image that grabs us—not with the cool impact of a great "idea," but as a hot sensation that goes instantly to the pit of our stomach.

It carries us to a tiny platform far above the safety of the floor we nervously leave behind. A bar awaits. There is no net. Just a catcher's hands. "He'd better be there!"

But we are forced to push the envelope farther. Our catcher can't be seen. We are asked to free fall into invisible hands. We have only his word—and his record—that he'll be there, that we have heard his invitation correctly.

It is far from easy. We are not a trusting people. We are in fact people taught that lack of trust is a sign of maturity. We laugh uneasily at the story of the father who coaxes a child to jump into hands that are at the last moment withdrawn. "That'll teach you to trust no one!" We laugh, but we get the point, and part of us, maybe all of us, buys the message and socks it away for a rainy day.

It haunts us at this moment, when free of the platform and the bar, we entrust our life and hope to the strong hands of an unseen catcher.

There is something else to remember. In the world of the circus the flyer is a star who brings to his moment in the air a lifetime of skills and practice. His timing has become perfect. He has been here many times before.

We are amateurs, Sunday gymnasts, awkward, inexperienced, our timing lousy.

We are, in another Nouwen insight, more a clown than a flyer.

The chances of our soaring gracefully through a "triple" into waiting hands are slight.

We are more likely to stumble off our platform, more likely to release our hold on the bar with arms, legs, and soul flailing. We are not in a position to seek out the waiting hands. We can't see them. He will have to catch us where we are, where we fall.

In the end our spiritual journey is not *our* story. It's the catcher's story.

"We're going to be caught. We're going to be safe. The great hero is the least visible. Trust the catcher."

Meanwhile send in the clown that we are.

Henri J. M. Nouwen
(1932-1996)

In our time very few western spiritual teachers have caught our imagination as profoundly as did the Dutch-born priest Henri Nouwen who died at the age of sixty-four in 1996.

Perhaps this was so because he was an original thinker (he taught at Notre Dame, Yale, and Harvard) and prolific writer (some thirty books). Perhaps it was because he was that rare teacher who could uncover great spiritual truths in the flight of an acrobat and the antics of a clown. But most likely it was because he never hesitated to expose his humanity. We were at ease with him because he was at ease with us, even when he was not at ease with himself.

Theology and psychology enriched his life and his writings, but his words and insights seldom moved far from the experiences of his personal spiritual journey. At the time of his death someone who knew him well said that his books were an ongoing story of what he wanted to be. Many times he wrote convincingly of a spiritual life he could not quite live. "Not quite . . ." is an experience we know well and which we probably unconsciously recognized in the warm sympathetic character of his writings. He might dazzle with showmanship and talk to citizens of several continents in a week's time, but what he said made him one of us.

Two of his friends, fellow spiritual directors, tell of writing polite replies to a young man pushing them for advice. Henri's way was to invite the writer to move in with him for a month. But most telling perhaps was that he spent the last years of his life as a pastor of L'Arche Daybreak near Toronto, a community where people with developmental disabilities and their friends live together. While there he developed a deep friendship with Adam Arnett, a man who never spoke a word and to whose basic needs Henri tended.

Henri Nouwen was a very modern man who came to know, despite overwhelming success, how indiscriminating depression is and how deep it can reach. He was someone who would pick up his telephone at all hours to reach across continents to talk with a friend, not because they needed him, but to admit that he needed them.

People read him not just because they are at ease with him, but because his transparent humanity makes his spiritual insights trustworthy. He, in turn, flew freely because he was confident that there was someone to catch him.

I

The clown saves us.

—HENRI NOUWEN

As much as he admired the trapeze artists, Henri Nouwen's heart was with the clowns. With us.

The clown saves us from convincing ourselves that only spiritual trapeze artists with their superb timing can ever find God.

The clown gives hope to the rest of us who are not at "the center of the events." Like us, clowns "fumble and fall." They "don't have it all together, they do not succeed in what they try, they are awkward, out of balance, and left-handed."

Clowns are like us—who trust that when we approach God we will not find a sign that says: "Only trapeze artists, only the gifted, only the unbroken need apply."

We are looking for the sign that says: "Bring in the clowns—bring in the broken. . . ."

The clown saves us.

LET US PRAY

As this night begins,
I pray that you will
make room in your heart
for one more clown—
someone who doesn't have it all together
(who never has)
who is awkward in your presence.
and whose soul, it seems,
is always out of balance.
Find in my fumbling and falling
something to bless,
a tongue-tied prayer
to be heard.

2

Spiritual life is an enfleshed life.

—HENRI NOUWEN

It took Nouwen almost a lifetime before he could write in one of his final books: "There is no divine life outside the body."

Sharing with him as many of us do a heavy historical burden of disconnect between body and spirit we can understand and sympathize with Nouwen's long journey. We are on the same road that he traveled, but for many of us the end is still not in sight.

We don't trust the bodies that God gave us and which in the Christian tradition God assumed. We proceed on our spiritual journey half convinced that God didn't quite know what he was doing when he embodied our spirit. We take pious shelter in a belief that somehow the body God assumed was not like ours. His was mere costuming.

But if that body was as real as ours is, it means that to become intimate with God I have to be on loving terms with my body.

The spiritual life is an enfleshed life—or it is no life at all.

LET US PRAY

As this night begins,
help me to understand,
that I should look for you
in the last place
I would expect to find you.
I don't have to go anywhere.
You are here
in a body tired from a day's work,
and all the days that stretch out behind me,
in a body that finds new ways everyday
to remind me how fragile life is.
How strange of you
to wrap yourself
in weakness.

3

Nobody or nothing can live up to our absolutistic expectations.

—HENRI NOUWEN

Here is what we can expect.

We can expect in ourselves and in others moments of generosity and courage and bursts of unexpected self-lessness. Even patience with ourselves, with others, with God. And a moment later we can expect to fail. We can expect to stumble. We can expect to doubt. We can expect to fall short of what we want to be, of what we appear to be, of what we think we must be.

We can expect to be human. Which means that we can't expect perfection. We can't expect anybody or any-thing—including ourselves—to live up to absolutist expectations of perfection that we impose upon our-selves and others, thinking that it is only in escaping our frail humanity that we can live up to God's expec-tations of us.

But we can expect also to be surprised by grace because this too is part of our humanity. We can expect moments of unexpected peace. We can expect moments when our heart opens up, when we can see goodness where we have never seen it before. And we can expect glimpses of God in the most unexpected places at the most unexpected times.

Just don't expect to be other than human.

LET US PRAY

As this night begins,
put to rest my expectations
that finding you
will mean shaking off my humanity.
Help me to accept
that when I wake tomorrow
my body will still ache,
my heart will still be wayward,
my soul will still
settle for less than you promise.
I will still be human,
but you will still be with me.

4

Your heart is greater than your wounds.

—HENRI NOUWEN

Who can deny that we carry with us wounds too deep to be cured by even the best efforts of our mind? "Who but a God," as a classical poet wrote, "goes woundless all the way."

It is hard to accept that there is no talking away such wounds or explaining them out of existence. There are no miraculous cures for the soul. Healing it is not a matter of finding the right words for our pain or the right category for what ails our humanity.

Our wounded being must be taken to heart, that is to that place where God awaits us, that sacred center of our being, that meeting place where God is forever present and accessible.

Our heart is greater than our wounds, but even here our wounds are not healed. They remain as a badge of our inescapable humanity. We come to this place not in search of a cure, but in search of a God who offers love and acceptance to the wounded.

"Here I am, Lord, wounds and all—safe in your hands."

LET US PRAY

As this night begins,
I know that I have to trust
that you will be with me,
however broken and wounded my soul.
I do not have to earn your love,
I do not have to be healthy and whole.
I need only to remember
that my heart is greater than my wounds,
that you await me there
with your healing presence.

5

Ultimately we must choose between security...and freedom.

—HENRI NOUWEN

There is the security of the earth beneath our feet.

And there is the freedom of the flyer who leaves behind the security of the platform for the dramatic freedom of flight.

There is the security of the mask, the happy face, the other face that hides our fragility.

But there is the freedom of the clown, who exposes his fragile humanity with a painted face, baggy pants, and faltering steps.

There is the security of knowing what little we can know.

And there is the freedom of embracing the unknown that lies a step away from the platform.

There is the freedom of living our lives where security ends.

"Ultimately we must choose between security ... and freedom."

LET US PRAY

As this night begins,
I confess
that freedom frightens me.
I don't want to let go
of what little security I know.
There is a part of me that is
afraid of the dark,
part of me that does not quite believe
that if I let go, you will catch me.
Every time.
Trust does not come easily.
I know I must choose.
But be patient, I beg you,
with my hesitant soul.

Surrender

THÉRÈSE OF LISIEUX

It is through love alone
that we can become pleasing to God,
and the only way
that leads to Love's Divine furnace
is the way of self-surrender.
It requires the confidence of the little child
who sleeps without fear in its father's arms.
Through the mouth of Solomon
the Holy Spirit has told us:
"Whosoever is a little one,
let him come unto me.
To the one who is little
mercy is granted."

—THÉRÈSE OF LISIEUX

Surrender

Many—ourselves included?—presume faith to be the last refuge of someone unable to deal with the harsh realities of life in an unforgiving world. It seems obvious to them—unnervingly possible to us?—that faith is a flight, an escape, a retreat from reality.

To be told furthermore that surrender is the root of faith is to reinforce the conviction that the pursuit of God is the last refuge of cowards, of those not equal to life. Physical, emotional, and psychological courage of the kind recognized and celebrated by the world, we are forced to admit, is not our strongest suit.

But there is another kind of courage, different from that required to stare down the world and force it to accept your terms. There is the spiritual courage required to surrender your heart. There is the bravery that is required to let go of what is known, of what gives you security. There is the courage of faith.

It is the courage known to everyone who has ever fallen in love, who has ever put their heart in the hands of another, who has ever let down the walls of their soul to let someone else in.

There is still another kind of courage. This is a courage that is not dependent on our possessing overwhelming strength or irresistible power. It is the courage of someone who comes to God empty-handed and undeserving, without any pretense, knowing that he cannot conquer God, but only surrender. It is the courage of humility.

It comes hard to those who have come to trust the hard-won virtues of their adulthood to be told that they must be like little children. But that's the way it is. Faith is not about power. It is about weakness. It is about humility. It is about surrender. It is about being childlike.

"Truly; I say to you, unless you turn and become like little children, you will never enter the kingdom of heaven. But whoever humbles himself like this child, he is the greatest in the kingdom of heaven."

It is a very hard message that requires of us "the confidence of the little child who sleeps without fear in its father's arms."

This is not easy for those of us who cling to the belief that, even in the presence of God, we are all grown up.

Thérèse of Lisieux
(1873-1897)

Grown-up virtues are not something that Thérèse of Lisieux considered helpful to someone in search of God. Childhood virtues are.

She was born Thérèse Martin in Alençon, France in 1873. She entered a cloistered convent when she was fifteen and died nine years later. Her only contact with the world was a few letters to missionary priests.

Yet only thirty years later she was a canonized saint, a household name, without question the best known and best loved mystic of modern times. Her fame and attraction for millions were and still are rooted in an autobiography published in a somewhat sentimentalized version that sweetened the relentless darkness in which she had served and loved a God who persisted in remaining hidden behind veils impenetrable to anything but a faith as unfazable as hers. "You might think," she wrote, "that I am a child for whom the veil of faith is almost rent asunder. But it is not a veil. It is a wall which reaches to the very heavens, shutting out the starry skies."

In that darkness she came to know and treasure the basic spiritual truth of her life with God: "He gives himself not just to the great, but to the little child who knows nothing, and can utter only feeble cries."

Out of that darkness and sense of childhood's powerlessness she created, lived, and wrote of an enormously but deceptively easy and accessible mystical theology that would make her a Doctor of the Church— the faith that has come to be known as her "little way." She insists that we are, in our relationship with God, always very small children in need of being carried in the arms of our Father. That's okay, she taught, because there is no need to be anything else. More importantly, there is no way we can be anything else.

Those who believe they can earn and serve the companionship of God in the ways of adulthood need not apply.

It is a doctrine that puts surrender at the heart of faith.

It is a hard doctrine for those of us who have been educated to confuse sanctity with self-control, with a need to prove ourselves worthy, to be the masters of our spiritual fate, to be, even in the face of God, self-reliant.

She says: "surrender." She says: "let go." What you seek is veiled, is walled off from everything *you* can do. Don't parade your achievements. Let go of them.

It is called surrendering.

I

Jesus does not guide me openly.
I neither see nor hear him.

—THÉRÈSE OF LISIEUX

Thérèse's life was a walk in the dark. She never saw the Father she so trusted. She never heard his voice. But she was never in doubt about who was guiding her steps, whose lead she was following.

There is nothing unusual about this. In the end, all journeys of faith are in some basic, profound way like hers. They are taken blindly. They progress in silence. No exceptions. Our journey included.

It is, of course, not the way we would like it to be.

In our experience night walks can be dangerous when taken down seldom-used streets. We prefer crowded, well-lighted thoroughfares. But the path of faith has never been known as the best-lighted, safest street in town.

LET US PRAY

As this day passes into night,
I know that I may never in this life see you,
never hear your voice.
I may be destined
to walk always
in the dark.
But let me feel your presence
at my side,
and if this is not possible,
silently guide my steps
where you wish me to go.

2

I need not be great.
On the contrary, I must remain little.

—THÉRÈSE OF LISIEUX

Thérèse is in love with being "little."

After all, much less is expected of us when we are little. We need not prove to God over and over again how great and deserving we are. We are who we are. And it is enough for God.

The problem, of course, is that what is good enough for God is frequently not good enough for us. We're adults and we don't like building our sense of worth on undeserved gifts. We have a rather nasty word for clinging to childhood: regression.

We have been led to believe that life is all about qualifying for eternity, about piling up enough points to let us pass through to another life.

And along comes Thérèse saying in effect: get over your adult posturing.

Here's one place where merit badges don't count. But childlike faith does.

LET US PRAY

As this day passes into night,
remind me again
that I need not
posture in your presence.
Here, I am a child
and need not be anything else.
Let me lay aside
for this brief moment
everything I use to convince myself and the world
of my worth.
You need no convincing,
even though I do.

3

Think of yourself as a little child
just learning to stand on her feet.

—THÉRÈSE OF LISIEUX

It is not easy to accept oneself as dependent in a world that treasures only those who can stand on their own two feet.

But it's the nature of faith to reach out for a steadying hand.

And what is more important is recognizing and accepting the fact that you will always need that hand. You will never walk alone.

To submit to such dependence means abandoning the very characteristics on which we have long hung our claim to value and self-esteem. It is not easy to let go of what we have long trusted in order to put our lives in the hands of a God who demands absolute trust, absolute confidence.

But unless, Thérèse echoing the scriptures says, we become like little children eager to be taken by the hand, eager to borrow our strength from a loving father, unless we humble ourselves and forget that grown-ups need not apply, we will not enter the kingdom of heaven. We will never know what joy and strength there is in surrender.

LET US PRAY

As this day passes into night,
let me admit that I need someone to lean on,
someone to carry me.
not just through the darkness of this night
but in the brightest moments of my day.
Remove from my soul's vocabulary:
"Thank you very much, but I can do that.
I don't need anyone."
For unless I become
like a little child,
eager and willing to take your hand,
I shall never enter into the kingdom
you have promised.

4

I hope for as much from the justice of the Lord as from his mercy.

—THÉRÈSE OF LISIEUX

The last thing most of us want from God is justice. Better for us, we think, that he have a blind eye and a faulty memory.

But our true hope is in God's perfect vision of who we are, and his faultless memory for the kind of creatures he made, walking monuments to imperfection.

Our fear of justice goes back to our unspoken belief that in order to come before God we must qualify. It can't be done. And as long as we insist on approaching God and responding to his advances with purely human standards, we will see ourselves as objects of pity rather than the objects of God's unconditional love.

God knows who we are and what we are capable of.

God's justice is the best friend our feeble humanity could ever have.

Once again Thérèse stuns us with the profound simplicity of her insights.

LET US PRAY

As this day passes into darkness,
wrap my days and nights
in your justice.
Let me sleep
soundly in your care.
I have nothing to fear from you,
but only from my insistence
on earning your love.
You know who I am,
and still
in your justice
you love me.

5

I just say what I want to say to God
and he never fails to understand.

—THÉRÈSE OF LISIEUX

The language of our soul is God's mother tongue.

God does not need translators to understand the words of our soul. So why do we think we need them?

Why is it so hard for us to trust the words that arise most naturally from our soul? Why do we reach so quickly for formulas? Why do we presume that God prefers dead words rescued from prayerbooks for the words that we share with friends? Why do we so often presume that the passionate, troubled, joyous, anxious, stuttering language of our soul is not suitable for the ears of God?

It is almost as though we think that God would prefer us to be someone else, that who we are is not good enough to be in his presence, not good enough to be caught up in his love.

It's as though God would prefer the company of giants to the company of children content to be caught up in his arms, dependent on his strength.

Thérèse always knew better.

LET US PRAY

As this day passes into night,
hear the silent yearning of my soul.
I have no other language.
I need no other.
For I do not know
what I want to say,
or even what I truly want.
My soul is tongue-tied,
but more eloquent
than I know.
Hear me.

Heart

BLAISE PASCAL

The heart has its reasons
which the reason knows not.
It naturally loves the Universal being,
and loves itself naturally according to the
measure in which it gives itself
to one or the other—
to reason or to God.
And it hardens itself against
one or the other as it pleases.
It is the heart that is conscious of God
and not the reason.
This then is faith:
God sensible to the heart,
not to the reason.

—BLAISE PASCAL

Heart

Behind our need to know there is an even deeper and more subtle hunger for a kind of certainty that is the nemesis of faith.

It's a hunger that faith cannot satisfy because unlike the works of reason, unlike mathematics and science, it deals with the unknowable and unprovable. It deals with mystery.

Pascal, one of the great mathematicians of his generation, knew this well. The believer is someone who chooses, like him, to live in tension, suspended, as Anthony Levi has said of him, between "darkness and light, knowledge and ignorance, greatness and wretchedness, doubt and certainty, anxiety and boredom, fear and confidence."

It is to live with mystery, with the competing and paradoxical claims of heart and reason.

This is not a description of faith that is welcomed and cherished by those of us who harbor the hope that in the discovery of God, by virtue of faith, we will forever be free of doubt and ambiguity.

But it is a truth to be embraced by anyone seeking to live a life of faith compatible with our radical finitude, our defining limitations, our agonizingly restricted humanity.

We are not destined for intellectual certitude.

Faith does not make God a sure thing. Just—in the provocative insight of Pascal—a "good bet." Our best bet. A risk worth taking. The ultimate risk.

Faith is a roll of the dice that begins with heart.

That risk has for the last three centuries been called Pascal's wager. Betting on God still has its original power to shock and upset the easy complacency of the believer and challenge the every bit as smug security of the unbeliever.

Our reason cannot tell us with certainty whether or not there is a God, or what such a God might be, only that this roll of the dice has infinite potential.

In faith, "you bet your life."

If this image makes you uncomfortable, try another that means the same. Take a leap of faith. Walk on water.

Blaise Pascal
(1623-1662)

Beginning at 10:30 on the evening of November 23, 1654 and for the next two hours Blaise Pascal had a life shaping experience of God. He forgot "all the world and all things, except only God."

In that moment he surrendered to his heart.

It is not the sort of surrender that you expect to find in the life of a scientist and inventor of historic stature whom biographers with good reason have called "one of the greatest minds of modern intellectual history . . . one of the most universal geniuses of modern France." On that night in 1654 he was just thirty-one years old, but he had already created the first calculator, become known for his contributions to conical theory and then gone on to disprove the impossibility of vacuums.

But now his heart had found reasons that his formidable reason knew not.

It was not a question for him of abandoning reason, for that would be to abandon his humanity. He would never forget that "a human being is only a reed, but he is a thinking reed." "All our dignity," he wrote, "consists of thought." He never surrendered that dignity.

But he also knew that reason can take us only so far. Not far enough to satisfy our hunger for God. It is the heart that must finish the journey.

It is a hard distinction for us to grasp, a hard priority to embrace in an age that equates "heart" with unbridled sentimentality, and reason with scientific certainty.

There is nothing sentimental, however, about Pascal's "heart." It is the core of our drive to escape, however enthralling and central, the limits and promises, the equations of our reason.

It is the source of the energy we require for the spiritual journey.

It is that in us which naturally loves the Universal being. And seeks it out.

It is that in us which is conscious of God. And responsive.

I

It is the heart that is conscious of God
and not the reason.

—BLAISE PASCAL

It was the English scholar and writer Ronald Knox who said that the primary value of rational proofs for the existence of God was to let you go back to sleep after waking at four in the morning with the unsettling thought that God might not exist. They are also useful for protracting late night discussions into early morning profundities.

Even the most rational among us, however, is disinclined to shape our life on the outcome of a syllogism or someone else's superior late-night debating talents.

That's not the door through which God enters our lives and gets a hearing.

It is the heart that makes us conscious of God.

We are not talking Valentine's Day or license plate hearts announcing someone's love for New York.

We are talking about the life that begins within, where our best efforts leave off, where our mind admits to a world beyond its comprehension and the heart must take over, where reason admits its limits and steps aside for what alone the heart can know.

The heart's knowledge is called faith.

LET US PRAY

As this day passes into night,
let me leave behind
the world where I'm expected
to answer every question
and solve every problem,
where I am expected to prove myself
over and over again.
Remind me of my limits.
Let my heart take over,
even as you take over my heart.

2

Shall I believe that I am nothing?
Shall I believe that I am God?

—BLAISE PASCAL

A great temptation for someone taking their first steps on the spiritual journey is to search out the easy comfort of extremes.

Some days we want to renounce passion and become Gods. On other days we want to renounce reason and become brutes.

"I am worthless or I am divine."

These polar opposites attract because they erase complexity. They avoid ambiguity. They free us from a demanding journey through the messy middle ground where we are neither worthless or God, but human with a touch of both.

It is a choice that is often aided and abetted by the inflamed language of spiritual teachers who speak in the superlatives of perfection and damnation.

Neither is our spiritual home.

We are something wonderful. But we are not God.

We are wounded. But it is not terminal.

We are just flawed creatures meeting God in the imperfect land that is our home.

LET US PRAY

As this day passes into night,
I have no tales of great success or failure
to bring you.
Just ordinary memories of an ordinary day—
reminders that I am neither worthless nor divine,
just one more flawed creature
bone weary at the end of a day
with its thousand ordinary moments.
Here in the silence
hear my ordinary prayer.
Bind up my wounds.
Let me feel welcome.
Tell me that you have been waiting for me
here in the dark.

3

Happiness is neither outside us
nor within us.

—BLAISE PASCAL

"It is both outside and within us," Pascal would say. "It is in God." He recognizes our taste for locatable happiness, for a "manageable" God, our very human temptation to pin God down so as to more easily put our happiness where we can lay our hands on it.

But happiness is not "out there" or "in here." It is not in the world around us or in the spirit within us. It is neither here nor there. It is where the inside and the outside meet and dissolve into each other, where words like "in . . . out . . . here . . . there" are meaningless.

It is where our heart finds God, where faith takes us.

Our happiness, Pascal reminds us, is a matter of the heart and not the reason. It is a matter of faith, not geography.

Because it is neither here nor there, our happiness is always close to hand, close to heart.

It is always here. It is always now.

It is never a matter of "I could be happy if only I were somewhere else."

LET US PRAY

As this day passes into night,
I am where I am.
To be here in the silence and dark
of this fading day
is good enough for you.
I need not look
for some other more spiritual place,
some other more convenient time.
You are not here rather than there,
Not later rather than now.
You are where my heart is.
Here. Now.

4

We want truth
and find only uncertainty in ourselves.

—BLAISE PASCAL

Here is the irony: in our desire to find God, in our determination to walk a spiritual path we have to be careful not to trip over the ambiguities and paradoxes that come with and define our fault-prone humanity.

"We are unable," Pascal wrote, " not to want truth and happiness, but we are incapable of either certainty or happiness."

Recognizing and accepting what we cannot be, what we cannot do, provides a reality check for those of us who might hope that the spiritual journey is a passport out of the human condition. We'll never be God. The moment that we accept this, we are on our way to spiritual wisdom and happiness rooted in the most profound truths of our human existence and God's attraction to us as we are. Our spiritual journey will not grind to a halt at every evidence that we are still human.

Our days, our hearts are destined to be stretched like Pascal between "darkness and light, knowledge and ignorance, greatness and wretchedness, doubt and certainty, anxiety and boredom, fear and confidence." We will be forever human.

So be it.

LET US PRAY

As this day passes into night,
teach me how to find you,
how to live with you
in twilight,
in those places,
where it is neither dark nor light,
in those hours
when it is neither day nor night.
My soul yearns for the certitude
of one or the other.
I want to hold on to light
that is never bright enough
and even now is fading.
I am not ready to embrace the dark.
Embrace me where I am.

5

Our nature is not to go forward all the time. It has its to's and fro's.

—BLAISE PASCAL

We prefer straight, unrelentingly, upward paths and the slightest dip is often enough to throw us into confusion.

We diet for eight days and fill up on the ninth and then berate ourselves as though the eight days don't count, as though they never happened.

"Look at me. I'm a failure. How come? I was doing so well."

And the answer comes back: "Because it's in our nature to forever gain a little, and forever to lose a little. Life has a lot of two steps forward and one step back."

The spiritual journey is no exception, because we make that journey as who we are . . . human beings . . . not as what we would like to be, escapees from a frail, inconstant humanity.

For eight days we set aside time for prayer. And on the ninth we set aside time for a mindless sitcom.

But the journey is all the steps, even the backward ones. It's not in our nature to go forward all the time.

It's certainly not what God expects. So why are our expectations higher than God's?

LET US PRAY

As this day passes into night,
I won't bother to count
the forward and backward steps of this day.
They don't matter.
You are forever where I am
wherever I will be.
You beckon me forward.
You are there to catch me when I fall.
"It is not in our nature to go forward all the time."
It is certainly not in mine.
I'll just have to get used to it . . .
to your way of doing things,
to your expectations,
not mine.

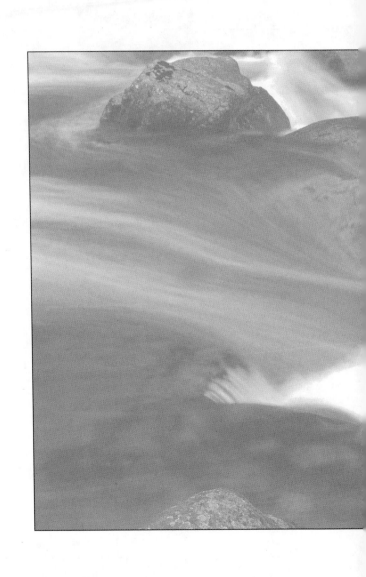

Loving God

AL-GHAZZALI

As for the signs of a man's love for God,
let it be borne in mind
that everybody claims his love,
but few really love him.
Beware of self-deception;
verify your statement by introspection.
Love is like a tree
rooted in the garden
sending its shoots above the starry heaven;
its fruit is found in the heart,
the tongue and the limbs of the lover—
in fact, his whole self
is witness to love,
just as smoke is a sure sign
of a burning fire.

— ALI NAWAB

Loving God

At a time when football players thank their buddy Jesus for the winning extra point and politicians grate-fully—and of course humbly—acknowledge their divine selection and coronation, the clear-eyed per-spective of Islam is a refreshing reminder that God deserves better than this trivialization.

God is omnipresent, all knowing . . .
God is the originator of the heavens and
the earth;
and wherever God decrees anything
God says to it, "Be!"
And it is.

God is the inescapable, unreduceable center of Islam. A spirituality without an omnipotent God as its center is radically unimaginable and unacceptable to them. This means that a spirituality centered on any-thing but unfathomable mystery misses the point.

It is an important reminder.

We have fallen into a habit of talking about God as though he were one of the boys, as though we know what we are saying. We don't. God too easily becomes little more than "the official spokesperson" and valida-tor of whatever value system we chose to canonize. He is the "Spirit of America"—or good old Elmdale High—on hand for ceremonial occasions and those times when gloating over personal triumphs would seem to be in bad taste.

These are gross examples, of course, and the easy target of cheap shots. But we are all capable of trying to bend God to our own dimensions.

We speak of love between God and us, as though we knew what it meant. But we don't. We talk as though it were love between equals—the only kind we understand. As a consequence we end up looking for and expecting all the wrong things from a love that knows no comparisons. We fall in love with what we know, but when we claim to love God it is a matter of surrendering to what we don't know.

What we can say about our relationship to God is bound by the same limitations that we face when we attempt to say anything about God. We can only know and speak of what God is not. We can only know and speak of what loving her is not.

Putting God back in the center of our spirituality is, therefore, not a matter of "getting our arms around" an idea—or even a person. It is a matter of letting go of any desire to capture God. Or define God's love.

Al-Ghazzali
(1058-1111)

Great spiritual teachers—and their wisdom—survive not just the test of time, but the test of translation into other traditions and cultures. Al-Ghazzali (Abu-Hamid Muhammad Al-Ghazzali) passes both tests. In his own time he read the great Christian theologians who wrote in the tradition of Greek philosophy. After ten centuries, during which he has influenced major western thinkers as disparate as Aquinas, Dante, and Pascal, he is still being read far beyond the perimeters of Islam.

But his impact on Islamic spirituality is the heart of his importance. As an influential teacher at major academic centers he attracted fine minds. As a writer of such works as "The Revival of Religious Sciences" he was responsible for bringing Sufism into the mainstream of Moslem orthodoxy and making mysticism an acceptable and primary part of Islam's spiritual life and appeal.

It was this very success, however, that shaped his own personal growth. He had begun his career as an academic theologian with a reputation for wide reading, openness of mind, and extraordinary originality of thought. With it came fame and spiritual dissatisfaction. He fled academe to become a pilgrim who prayed at Mecca, Medina, Jerusalem, and Hebron. The philosophy he studied and taught had become an enemy of Iman, the faith he treasured. He chose not to follow and teach a path of disputatious philosophy and religious law but rather one of ecstatic experience.

The story of Al-Ghazzali is a conversion story, as accessible today as it was ten centuries ago.

But it is also a story of changing times. Today his work and ideas are missing from the academic syllabi in many Moslem countries. Too much Christian influence, it is said. Too many impurities. It is also highly unlikely that very many Christian theology students have read him. The openness that fueled and energized his thought and the religious world centuries ago has given way to sectarian suspicions and spiritual isolationism.

When he died in his home town of Tus (in present-day Iran) in 1111 he left behind him over 400 works that embraced not just theology and asceticism but poetry, music, songs and dance—and a slip of paper on which he had written: "Praise be to God who has now set me free."

I

The essence of religion is love.

—AL-GHAZZALI

When he wrote these words Al-Ghazzali meant them to be a corrective, a challenge to the status quo of Islam and of his own practice. Too often religion had become a jousting ground for law (which he felt had no place in religion) and disputatious scholarship (which warred with faith). It still seems that way to many who deny interest in religion and opt for spirituality. When he first identified love as the essence of religion it still had the power to shock. Now it sounds like one more version of religion as a heart-warming glob of sentimentality.

Even if the statement "The essence of religion is love," has not been entirely drained of meaning by time and misuse, certainly its power to shake up our soul and the world of religion is gone. But for Al-Ghazzali these words became the driving force behind the conversion that would shape the remainder of his life.

It was an insight and a conviction strong enough to uproot him from a life of accomplishment and fame and to pursue years of pilgrimage and prayer that would end in a return to the simple life of the town where he was born. It was an insight that would bring him home again.

LET US PRAY

As this night begins,
it seems too easy
to say that religion is love—
as though love were too easy a way
of seeking and serving you.
But love is never easy
for a heart like mine.
I am much too afraid
to let go of my petty securities,
to place my trust in you.
But here in the dark,
let me try.

2

Lovers meet with fears that are unknown to others.

—AL-GHAZZALI

Love is not a refuge, a cocoon, a security blanket for the soul.

Anyone who has ever sought shelter in love knows better, knows it exposes the soul, knows it lets fear in.

There is the fear of disappointing the one you love.

There is the fear of an impenetrable veil.

There is the fear of being turned away.

But there is a greater fear—the fear of never having surrendered to the only love that could measure up to the longings of your heart. So to make room for love you welcome fear.

You will never measure up if you use only your own measurements.

There will always be more behind the veil.

But this is certain. You will not be turned away.

LET US PRAY

As this night begins,
I am afraid of babbling easy words,
and being turned away
for lack of the love
that will gain entrance to your heart.
Love is never satisfied with itself,
never measures the one you love,
or so it seems to me here in the dark.
But take, I ask of you,
what I can give,
however poor it seems to me,
however short it falls of what
I would like it to be.

3

Hope with fear should be the guide of love.

—AL-GHAZZALI

Love driven by fear alone will end in paralysis because we will shrink our God to manageable size.

Love driven by hope alone will overstep its bounds by losing sight of the undefinable mystery at the core of our journey.

But when our love—when our religion—is tempered by both fear and hope, God remains God and our prayers are neither craven nor arrogant. We can accept the evil around us without despair and recognize the good without presumption. We can accept the infinitude of God and the finitude of self without abandoning either.

But it's not easy to do. For though God remains God, we remain human. The mood of our soul swings with the unpredictability of our humanity and the roller coaster world in which we exercise our love.

Both fear and hope are at work.

But God knows what to expect from us.

LET US PRAY

As this night begins,
I can feel
the fear and hope that are at work
in my soul.
I pray because I hope in your love.
I hesitate because I am afraid to come before you
as who I am.
You are God.
I am so completely, utterly human.
Take me for what I am,
I cannot be anything else.
But it is enough.
I hope.

4

There is no God but God.

—AL-GHAZZALI

The temptation is to believe that once we have uttered the words we are living the reality.

It is not enough to announce, "there is no God but God," unless we understand what a radical change it implies in how we live. Otherwise we invite crippling self-delusion. Had Al-Ghazzali been writing in our own times he might have said: there is a vast difference between talking the talk and walking the walk.

It's a distance that is easily overlooked in our understandable desire for "instant God." But getting the words right will never be enough. For most for us the spiritual journey will be cluttered with a pantheon of Gods who are not God and clearing our soul of all the pretenders will be the work of a lifetime.

God is forever having "strange Gods" put before him.

Our task is to call them by their right name.

LET US PRAY

As this night begins,
I know
that there is no God but God,
no God but you,
but for me it is easier said
than lived.
The other Gods who clutter my heart
demand so little of me.
You want all of me.
Do not, I beg of you,
Overwhelm my heart.
Be patient with me
while my heart stretches
to match my words.

5

Let our hearts speak, let our deeds proclaim it, but not our tongues.

—AL-GHAZZALI

The language of God lovers must be long on deeds and short on words of self-congratulation.

Proclamations of personal salvation, of membership in some exclusionary club ring hollow when they smack of God choosing some of the race to love while overlooking others as though there were a spiritual class system.

God's love is universal. Our God-loving is to mirror that universality and to speak it in the movements of our hearts and in our deeds. God is not into distinctions. For her there is neither male nor female, Greek nor Roman. There is no thanking God that we are unlike the "others"—better than the rest. There is no standing in the front of the temple taking spiritual bows for our virtue, accepting congratulations for our election to a circle of insiders.

The language of God loving is spelled out in homeless sheltered, hungry fed, the naked clothed.

There is no call for words.

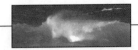

LET US PRAY

As this night begins,
there is a part of my heart
that wants to find its way
to the front of the temple,
part of my heart that wants you to know
that I am not like the others.
Remind that part of me
that you will be looking for me,
not there,
but in the back streets
of the city.

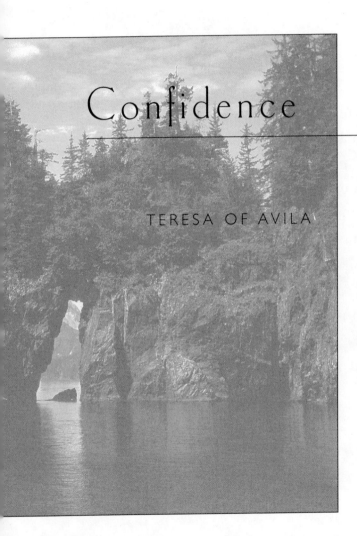

Confidence

TERESA OF AVILA

Because you are not only God,
but human also, you are not
surprised by our frailties.
You understand our nature.
You understand our habit of falling constantly.
And even though you are my Lord
I can therefore speak to you as a friend.
You are not like an earthly lord
who affects a power he does not have,
who is available only at fixed hours,
and with whom only certain persons may
speak.

—TERESA OF AVILA

Confidence

The use of the word "confident" to describe someone runs the risk of stirring up an image of strutting self-reliance.

It's a quality that seems to be at war with everything spiritual.

The spiritual seeker is stereotypically humble, not confident; diffident, even obsequious. It is hard to associate confidence with a bowed head and a bent knee.

But it belongs, because confidence is what faith is all about. Faith-based confidence is about living in unashamed reliance on someone who can be trusted with your life, to whom you freely and confidently "give your heart." This isn't self-assurance. It is faith. It is the admission that we can't go it alone and the recognition that we don't need to.

It is putting confidence in its place. Not in our vacillating heart but in the steadfast commitment of God to her creatures.

Our God "understands our nature" and is not "surprised by our frailties." Our God is not like some "earthly lord who affects power that he does not have, who is available only at fixed hours and with whom only certain people may speak." We will not be turned away because we come from the wrong side of the spiritual tracks.

The result is that we can come to God without apologies for who we are. We are, after all, his children and we come because we have been invited and assured of a welcome.

Knowing this puts confidence in our steps.

You won't find confidence, it is true, in any list of the virtues. The books never put it in the same class as prudence and fortitude.

Where you find it is in the life of someone like Teresa of Avila who approached God boldly, confident of a hearing, certain of support. "Do not be troubled," she wrote, "but hope in the Lord. If you pray and hope in the Lord and do what you can for yourself, God will bring about in your soul all that you desire."

You can be confident.

Teresa of Avila
(1623-1662)

She was a saint, a mystic, a no-holds-barred religious reformer and a world-class theologian who became the first woman ever to be named a Doctor of the Church.

Her brilliance has given her a place of honor in every theological library, but it has been something else that has established her over centuries in the hearts of spiritual seekers.

It has been her humanity.

There is something "old shoe" comfortable about this remarkable woman who could talk God-talk with the best of them, yet whose language steeped in the ordinary is enough to make the frailest, the most tongue tied of us feel at home.

The author of stunningly sophisticated treatises on the mystical mansions of the soul, she has entered the daily life of millions through her "bookmark"—a few lines that are accessible enough, memorable enough, and warm enough to end up on refrigerator doors and needlework samplers.

Like the Lord she prayed to, she is not surprised by our frailties. She understands our nature. She understands our habit of falling constantly. Like that same Lord she is not available only at fixed hours and to a "by invitation only" list of selected friends and fellow mystics.

She was born near Avila, Spain into the turbulent early years of the Reformation—she was two years old when Luther published his Ninety-five Theses. When she was twenty she entered a Carmelite monastery and spent the next twenty years prayerfully, but with a sense of being only half-alive.

Then in her late forties, in the wake of a profound religious conversion, she began the great works of her life. She undertook the successful reform of the Carmelite order in the face of religious, legal, and political opposition. She began writing her autobiographical and theological works. And she prayed. She became the most active of mystics, and the most mystical of activists.

A modern woman recognizes her on sight.

Everyone recognizes in her a model of confidence rooted in faith.

I

As God has a dwelling place in heaven,
so has he in the soul.

—TERESA OF AVILA

It is hard for us to take God at his word when he says
that it is his delight to dwell in the souls of men.

Some souls, we think, might delight him. Those souls
where you would expect to find God, where by our
standards we judge God might be comfortable. We
could understand that.

But it is not just "some" souls. It is all souls. At all
times. No exceptions. His word is good. None of us is
left out. None of us.

"As God has a dwelling place in heaven, so has he in
my soul." To believe this is to know, is to accept that
God is always as close as our next breath and wants to
be. It's hard to believe that God apparently thinks better of us than we do of ourselves.

But he says it is so. He invites our belief in his presence.
But he will not overwhelm us, nor compel our accept-
ance. There is nothing insistent or imperious about him.
Nothing. He is just "there" waiting to be recognized.

How ironic it is that we who seek God find it so diffi-
cult to believe that God has already found us, that we

live at this very moment in the presence of someone who wants to be with us, who is comfortable with us even when we are not comfortable with ourselves, with others or especially with a God who will not give up or go away.

LET US PRAY

As this night begins,
I want to believe
that you delight in my presence.
But such faith is hard for me.
There are hours, whole days, when
I cannot believe that anyone,
especially you, would want to be with me.
But I will take your word for it.
I will delight in your presence
and confidently
make a prayer
of my hope.

2

Blessed be he who can, when he pleases, draw good out of all my faults.

—TERESA OF AVILA

We can get to the point where when we look at our life all we see is a bundle of faults that add up to nothing much. A half-empty glass at best. Mediocrity, if we are left to our own devices, becomes the settled measure of our lives.

But God apparently is not, cannot be put off by the poverty of our soul. He sees something more. Something good can come of us. Something good can be spun out of the tangled skeins of our stumbling, half-hearted days.

"There's not much here to work with," we think, "but apparently God can make something of it." What that something might be only God knows, because the vision that God has of us is beyond every category we have ever used to measure our possibilities and our worth.

We are tempted to stay mired in our failures, to limit our lives to what we can imagine, to the security of what we are comfortable with. Left to ourselves, we strike a bargain with our faults and failings, believing them to be our destiny. But there is within our limitations, our faults and failures a divinely conceived creature waiting to be released, waiting to break through to a level of life only God can conceive.

To release that creature we will have to look beneath our feeble gestures to see what God sees—a heart desiring to desire and hoping to hope. We will have to borrow the eyes of God or forever be condemned to travel paths that lead nowhere but deeper into our own poverty.

"Blessed be he who can see in me what I cannot see." Our faith gives vision to that hope.

LET US PRAY

As this night begins,
draw good out of the faults and failures of this day.
Make something of the hope
that you have planted in my soul,
but which is still so fragile.
Let me see in the darkness
what only you can see.
Let me dream your dreams for me
and measure my soul
by the depth of your love
for what you find in me.

3

Let nothing disturb you.
Let nothing make you afraid.

—TERESA OF AVILA'S BOOKMARK

It's amazing how many of us think that being anxious and worried is a sign that we are spiritual, that we are committed, that we are not like everyone else, content to live on the surface of life.

According to this school of spirituality, there is nothing like a long face and a distracted soul, worried and busied by many things to demonstrate our spiritual depth! "Loving God is a very serious business. It's enough to bring on an ulcer."

There is also, apparently, according to this gospel of anxiety, nothing quite as spiritual as living our days in fear and trepidation, all but certain that our slightest misstep, our slightest unoccupied moment will cost us the love of God. The key to this kind of spirituality is to "stay busy" because it's all up to us.

The idea that we should just stand there in confidence while God does what only God can do, what in fact we can never do for ourselves, and what no amount of fear and anxiety can accomplish, is incomprehensible.

But then into the noisy, hassled center of our soul comes a voice of common sense, the truth of whose words we understand immediately and instinctively. "Let nothing disturb you. Let nothing make you afraid."

It's the voice of Teresa, but we hear another voice in another room: "Martha, Martha, you are anxious and troubled about many things, when only one thing is needed." Or from a mountainside we hear: ". . . do not be anxious about tomorrow, for tomorrow will be anxious for itself." And we hear an even more ancient voice that says: "Be still and see that I am God."

Be not disturbed. Stay still. There is nothing to worry about.

LET US PRAY

As this night begins,
let me be content to do nothing
but trust in you.
Let me put behind me
this day with all its worries and anxieties.
Let me be still.
Let nothing disturb me.
Let nothing make me afraid.
And in the stillness
Let me see that you are God,
and that you are here.

4

All things are passing,
God alone never changes.

—TERESA OF AVILA'S BOOKMARK

We wake to a day when God is so present to us that we can almost see his face and feel his breath. But this will pass.

We wake to another day when God is hidden from our sight no matter how urgent our hunger, no matter how we long for a hint of her presence.

But this too will pass.

One will take a second. Another will seem endless. Both will pass.

Our whole life will pass.

What will not pass, what never changes, is God.

We are never out of her sight, we are never unloved.

The more we change, the more God remains the same. It is the cornerstone of our hope. It is what makes our passing days livable.

LET US PRAY

As this night begins,
today will pass into darkness,
even as this night will become tomorrow.
Not all my clinging
can stop their passage.
Whatever *is*, except you,
will pass.
Help me to see beyond the passing moment.
Help me to live in hope
of what never changes.

5

If you have God
you will want for nothing.
God alone suffices.

—TERESA OF AVILA'S BOOKMARK

The tip-off to our need for God is that moment of emptiness when we finally have everything we ever wanted and needed, and it is not enough.

It is never enough.

There is nothing wrong with having "things" or wanting them.

But there is a problem when we delude ourselves into thinking that any thing, that any accumulation of things, will satisfy the hunger in the pit of our soul.

There is a problem when we bet our lives on things and come to believe that should we lose them there would be nothing left.

Teresa is saying that if at the end of the day we "lose everything" and have nothing left but God, it will be enough.

And God will be there, not as a replacement for what we have lost or surrendered, but as that for which there is no substitute and who alone is enough.

LET US PRAY

As this night begins,
help me to let go,
if only for these few hours,
of the "things"
that I relied on
to get me through this day.
Help me to put my confidence
in you
who will be there
even if I should lose everything.
I want more than anything else to believe
that you alone will suffice.
Help my unbelief.

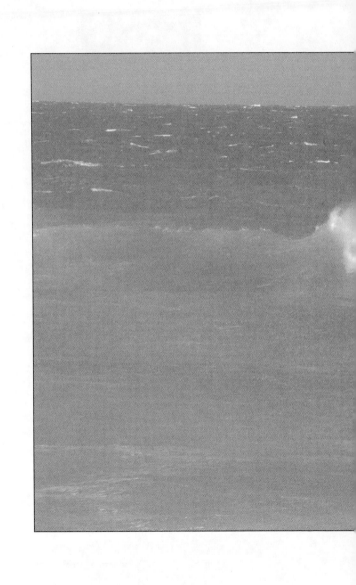

Wonder

PIRKE AVOT

You are walking lost in wonder,
emptied of self, and mindful of Reality,
and suddenly, you interrupt this peace
to exclaim:
"How beautiful is this tree!
How magnificent this field."
You forfeit the moment.
The intrusion of self
and the imposing of judgment
separates you from Reality
and snares you in a web of words.
Be still
and embrace it all in silence.

—RABBI JACOB

Wonder

Adult faith begins in childlike wonder.

It presumes an ease with mystery and a taste for what might be—a capacity for looking at the world and seeing what can't be seen.

But it is not a way of acting that sits smoothly with an adult. We are, after all, grown ups who tend to save our wonder for bedside stories best suited to toddlers. We pride ourselves on not falling prey to "what might be." We are realists and proud of it.

Nor is wonder a word you find frequently in spiritual literature. There is something too fantastical about it, something insubstantial and playful and childish about it. And theologians don't want to run the risk of confusing God with fairy tales.

But wonder is at the roots of faith, because it is the capacity to see the miraculous in the commonplace.

Without it we remain content with first impressions. We never permit what might be, what could be, and in the end what truly is to break through. We end up trapped in a small corner of reality that we can reach and control with our definitions and formulas.

We shut out mystery. We shut out the miraculous. And we lose sight of God.

We grow content with the surface of our world and our lives and miss the deep mystery that only wonder can release. "We walk in miracles," the poet Sister Maura wrote, "as children scuff through daisy fields," careless of the beauty that lies in our path and at our fingertips, unseeing of the God who waits for us at every step.

We walk with eyes wide shut and miss the daisies at our feet, the endless miracles within our sight, miracles that are as "common as spring, as bread, as sleep, as salt."

But when we miss God in the commonplace we miss her utterly. If we insist on looking for and finding God only in the exotic we miss the God at our fingertips.

"Oh deeper than daisy fields, we drown
in miracles, in God, our Seed, our Crown."

The Rabbis

(250-275)

The wise man who speaks in mysterious, often contradictory terms is common to nearly all the great religious traditions, but in the rabbinical traditions is represented by the Pirke Avot. The purpose is not to puzzle the hearer with gnostic insight but to deliver accessible, often gritty, enlightenment on how to live the good life.

It is a wise man who can speak plainly.

When in the middle of the third century of our Common Era the wise men brought together Pirke Avot, a classsic collection of rabbinical sayings, they could draw on wisdom and words that were first spoken and written as much as six centuries earlier.

The kind of material they gathered, commonsensical epigrams, came from an even older tradition, a form that bridged the cultivated wisdom of the rabbis and the needs of the least educated of their people.

In the tradition out of which Pirke Avot grew, the commonplace roots of spirituality meet the common sense needs of the soul. All souls. Not just the priviledged souls of scholars. At all times. Seventeen centuries later we can still recognize and live out its wisdom.

This may seem to be the obvious thing to do, but it flies in the face of whole traditions of special knowledge for special people, a notion that still has the power to capture our soul.

"Holiness is for others, the few, the blessed, the chosen."

But when we read the words of Pirke Avot—in whatever century we live—we find ourselves saying: "That makes sense. I can do that."

Centuries ago Rabbi Jacob said: "There is food all around you. If you go hungry it is because you ignore the banquet." Just a few years ago Patrick Dennis would have Auntie Mame say: "Life's a banquet and some poor bastards are starving."

Another Rabbi would say: "Wonder is the heart of life."

The wisdom of Pirke Avot travels well—nourishing faith as it goes.

I

Life is forever whispering its secrets.

—PIRKE AVOT

The secrets life whispers are lost to an inattentive heart.

"We are too busy to listen," says the Rabbi, "so we fail to hear anything but our own foolishness."

We become hard of hearing. We can't hear our heart ache. We pay attention neither to the voice of pain nor to the voice of beauty.

Life's whispered secrets escape us because it takes a silenced heart to hear a God who refuses to shout, who insists on whispering in a noisy world.

It takes an attentive heart not to miss the quiet voices of life as we pass by it and through it. So we end up with no place for the wonder in which faith can take root.

But the fact that we are not listening does not still the voice of God, does not dam up the secrets being whispered all around us. God speaks continuously even to those who are hard of hearing. Even when we are not paying attention.

"Be silent. Be still," the Rabbi says. "Listen and pay attention."

LET US PRAY

As this day passes into night,
into stillness,
into silence,
I will be as quiet
as my busy heart
will allow me.
I will listen for your secrets.
I will pay attention.
And I will whisper
secrets of my own
that I cover over
with the noise and light
of the day.
Hear me in this silence
in this darkness.

2

Miracles are the ordinary revealed in their simple splendor.

—PIRKE AVOT

A blade of grass is a blade of grass until it excites our wonder, until we sense in it the presence of God, until we hear in it the voice of God.

Then it is a miracle in all its simple splendor.

We are not talking miracles as magic. We are not talking "ooh and ah" engendering tricks. We are certainly not talking divine intervention in football games, political campaigns, or award ceremonies.

This is not a matter of "God on my side," or God seeking attention by dressing up her presence with fireworks.

We are talking about our everyday, ordinary world pregnant with mystery, awash in simple splendor.

A miracle occurs every time we look around and realize that there is more here than meets the eye.

The more is God.

LET US PRAY

As this day passes into night,
I thank you for all the miracles of this day,
the ones I recognized,
the ones I missed.
Even here in the night,
in the silence and the dark,
you are waiting for me.
Even in these moments
when I can hardly keep my eyes open
you are here.
Thank you
for the simple splendor
of this night
and the miracle of the sleep
that calls me.

3

We do not merit wonder
we simply open our eyes to it.

—PIRKE AVOT

The most startling discovery that we make on our spiritual journey is not the discovery of God, but the realization that he has been present all along.

The next startling discovery is a realization that not only have we done nothing to bring about this presence, there is in the end nothing we *can* do.

This is not like climbing Mt. Everest. It is not a matter of exercising a gigantic effort that in the end is rewarded by an extraordinary view. Wonder—a sense of God's presence—is not a reward. It is a gift given to us where we are.

Or we turn our eyes away. This is a choice that we are offered. This is within our power.

The view is available from where we are at this very moment.

There is nothing geographic about wonder.

There are no best seats for faith.

We simply open our eyes to the view that is ours for the accepting.

LET US PRAY

As this day passes into night,
I know that there is
a world of wonder
all around me in the dark,
if only I will open my eyes to it,
to you.
Let me see in the dark
with eyes
that you have opened for me.
Let me see the world
that you have given me.

4

Embrace it all in silence.

—PIRKE AVOT

Our task is to stay out of the way.

The Rabbi reminds us of moments when we have walked all lost in wonder. For a moment we were not filled up with "self." In its silence we were aware of a deeper, greater reality.

But then we become intruders with what at times seems like an insatiable need to take charge, to capture the moment with our words. It is almost as though God would not be present until we have named, described, and approved the occasion; until we have made it our own; until we have owned it; until we have given in to our need to capture God; until we have made faith unnecessary.

In that moment of intrusion we are separated from the wonder that captivated our soul. We are snared in a wordy web of our own making.

It need not be. We can continue our journey all lost in wonder.

We can keep our soul, if for only a moment, empty of self.

We can be still. We can embrace it all in silence.

LET US PRAY

As this day passes into night,
let me not forfeit
this moment of wonder.
Be still my heart,
and embrace the night
in silence.

5

Without wisdom there is no wonder.
Without wonder there is no wisdom.

—RABBI ELAZAR BEN AZARIAH

We are tempted to see wonder only in the eyes of a child and wisdom only in the eyes of the old.

But they belong together. In our eyes.

Wonder is about keeping our eyes wide open, like a child straining to catch every movement, every color, the comfort of every familiar face, and the thrill of every new face. It is about living in a world that demands exploration. Whether our world is as small as a crib or as vast as space, there's always more to see, to touch, and to feel. And it's all wonderful.

Wisdom comes early and stays late. It knows all about disappointment, about a world that promises much and too often delivers hardly at all, whether it is a toy that is always out of reach or a loved one who is no longer there. But it also knows the rewards of love cultivated and cherished. It knows about limitation, about not having everything, about the joys of what is possible. You can see it in the eyes of the wise.

Faith brings wonder and wisdom together. And keeps them together. It is a wise person who can keep looking at the world through eyes filled with wonder, who expects to find God at every turn, but who knows that God is always a surprise.

LET US PRAY

As this day passes into night,
let me admit to you and to myself
that too often my eyes are clouded over
and I miss the wonder of the day.
I mistake weariness for wisdom.
I am more likely to say
"enough is enough"
than to reach out for more.
Be patient with me
when I close my eyes
and cease to wonder.
Let me be wise enough
to open them again.

Silence

THE CARTHUSIANS

Let all my world
be silent in your presence, Lord
so that I may hear what you may say
in my heart.
Your words are so softly spoken
that no one can hear them,
except in deep silence.
But to sit alone and listen in silence
is to rise completely above our natural powers;
it is to rise above our selves.

—GUIGO II

Silence

For many of us, most of the time, silence is just a welcome absence of noise or an absence of others. The kids are in bed. The TV is off. The phone has stopped ringing. Our space in the world, if just for a moment, loses its noisy patina. In the "peace and quiet" we can for a moment, as a mother would say, hear ourselves think. Maybe even hear ourselves pray.

It's "God time"—the quiet corner of our lives that the prayer books say we should seek out.

But even as the night washes away the surface noise another layer of our day insists on being heard from. The outer quiet of the room gives way to the unquiet of our soul. The worries, the aches, the angers, the surprises, and the joys that were collecting just beneath the surface press on us, demanding to be recalled into being. Our world is very much with us, waiting with every passing moment to make its presence known. There seems to be no escape. Quiet beckons us from one step beyond every layer of our being only to slip through our fingers.

We are tempted to blame ourselves as though there must be something missing in our search for quiet. But it is the same for a kneeling monk at dawn as it is for a bone-tired single mother when the dishes are finally done. Inner quiet does not come readily to any of us. It can seem disturbingly elusive. It can seem at any given moment that we will never hear the voice of God whose words, Guigo tells us, are "so softly spoken that no one can hear them except in the deep silence" that seems forever to escape us.

Does this mean we shall never hear God's voice? No, only that we will not hear it until we understand that the softly spoken words of which Guigo speaks are the soft-center of our noisiest day.

The silence in which God can be heard is not the mere absence of noise, or the absence of others. The child at long last quietly in bed three rooms and a floor away is never more present, never speaks more clearly than in the quiet of the night. What is most important about that child, what God most wants us to hear, has a chance to be heard.

The key is not to drown out his voice with our words.

Only in stillness can we know that the voice we hear is God.

The Carthusians

In charterhouses (their word for monasteries) around the world (including Vermont) there are monks and nuns living today a spiritual way that goes back over nine hundred years to the time of Guigo and beyond. They are the Carthusians.

They are still held together by a conviction spelled out by Guigo: it is in silence and solitude that we find God. What makes them special as contemplatives is that they live out this conviction as solitary hermits who carefully guard and enjoy a saving touch of community life. Living alone typically in small four room, two-story hermitages, they emerge regularly for common events and prayers. Over the centuries this combination has exerted an attraction on saints and mystics from John of the Cross to Thomas Merton.

And let's admit it: at the end of the day it is a combination that that even the most worldly of us can envy without any real danger of our running off to join their ranks. We would like to venture if only for a moment into the solitude they occasionally leave behind. We are slated on the contrary to do our searching where silence is a rare commodity and even a moment of solitude a dream deferred more often than not by a constant companion—the needs of others and our obligation to meet them as best we can.

In the face of such reality do twelfth century monks committed to solitude and silence have anything to say to us? Isn't their wisdom born and nurtured in what appears to us to be a hothouse of unimaginable spiritual luxury, irrelevant to the hardscrabble dailiness of our search for a glimpse of God?

If all we see of them is their solitary cell and the almost unbroken silence of their days, we will miss the heart of their spiritual struggle—and ours—which is to silence not the noise around us but the noise within. This noise is of our own making, born of our feeling that we have to do the talking.

The point of our search for silence is not to "get a word in edgewise," but to let God make her presence known at the center of even the noisiest day of our lives and the noisiest hour of that day.

God doesn't wait for us to join him for a quiet weekend in the country. A chaotic day in the city will do just fine. God may very well be present in Carthusian silence and solitude, but he is no less present in a cluttered kitchen.

"Sit down and be quiet."

"Give silence a chance!"

We need to understand this if we are to hear what a secluded monk of the twelfth century has to say to a twenty-first century heart.

I

To sit alone and listen in silence
is to rise above our selves.

—GUIGO II

The idea of sitting alone and listening in silence stirs up images not just of secluded monastery cells but of lazy summer afternoons. It speaks of Adirondack chairs and hammocks, of a novel open on our lap to page one, of eyes more often closed than open, of sounds no louder than rustlings of nature.

It speaks of the soul at rest, free for the moment of the ordinary nuisances of being alive, the persistent annoyances of the day.

Rising above our selves is not in the air. No challenge is.

But our summer afternoon shares a secret with the twelfth century monk's contemplative vision.

We both know that without such moments of silent sitting and unforced listening there would be voices that we would never hear, visions we would never glimpse. Without them we would drown in the thousand deadening details that can so easily swallow our lives.

For in silent sitting it is not so much that we rise above our self, as it is that we discover our self in the voices heard and the visions glimpsed. It is a place where faith feels at home.

LET US PRAY

As this night begins,
let me set aside
the thousand deadening details
of this day
that still seem
ready to swallow up my life.
Let me spend this night
in silent, patient listening.
for what I would otherwise not hear.
Speak Lord.

2

No one can be at peace
until he has become humble.

—GUIGO II

There is no question that for most of us venturing into the presence of God is visiting another country where we are deathly afraid of not knowing the language.

We are even more afraid that he won't understand ours. And still more afraid that we will embarrass ourselves by the triviality of our efforts at prayerful "conversation."

"What in the world do you talk about?" And we dig about in dusty pages of approved topics and attitudes hoping to find the right things to say, hoping that God will find us interesting. So we go "to and fro talking of Michelangelo."

When indeed the sounds of silence will do just fine. After all, the substance of our prayer is and will always be that which escapes our understanding. Prayer is about going where words cannot take us.

So we say what we want to say or say nothing at all with the confidence of faith that our stuttering, our silence, our very selves will not fail to be understood.

LET US PRAY

As this night begins,
let me be content
with syllables of silence,
unembarrassed by my humanity
and unafraid of the dark.
Help me to feel at home
in this other country
where whatever I say
or leave unsaid
is heard and understood.

3

By myself I am a crowd.

—GUIGO II

There is something romantic, something we are inclined to think of as especially spiritual, about the lone figure walking an otherwise deserted beach, the cowled monk at his isolated prayer bench. "That would be nice."

Such images of solitude appeal to that part of the soul that wants to be alone, that harbors a conviction that God is most likely met when no one else is around. But such solitude is an illusion. The figure on the beach, the monk in his cell are not alone.

We are never that alone. Even "by myself I am a crowd," Guigo wrote.

There was for him a crowd of wild beasts that he nourished from childhood, who built their lairs in his soul and would not leave him alone. He had his demons. We have ours. He had his better angels. We have ours. But with or without demons and angels one thing is certain: we do not come to our moments of quiet without our history.

All our years will walk the beach with us and kneel at our side.

So too will God. This is certain.

We can trust the word of someone who wanted nothing more than to be alone—solitude is a crowded place.

LET US PRAY

As this night begins,
let me remember
that I am not going alone
into its darkness and quiet.
But for these few hours
let all my world,
all the voices of the crowd,
be silent in your presence, Lord.
Let me hear
what you want to say
to my heart.

4

He who is not silent cannot hear
when you speak to him.

—GUIGO II

Perhaps it is because we think of faith as a God-*search*
that we so often miss the central truth of our spiritual
journey. God is not at the end of some twisting road.
He's at the beginning and at every step along the way.
We don't have to go looking for God; we don't have to
search for God, no matter how distant she may seem to
be. God is already present. It is a question of getting out
of her way, of removing the layers of self-absorption
and self-importance that in the name of spirituality we
insist on establishing between him and us.

And this includes, in the name of prayer, talking too much.

Until we learn to be quietly content in the presence of
God we won't hear a word that is being spoken to us.

Until we really believe that remaining speechless is our
most effective prayer, we will forever be caught behind
a sound barrier that even God cannot penetrate.

Silence is faith's paradoxical mother tongue.

LET US PRAY

Let this night begin and end
in silence.
For once let me not try
to catch your attention
with my words.
Otherwise I will surely miss
what you want me to hear,
what you will speak softly
in my heart.
Help me to be content
To speak the silent language of faith.

5

Let all my world
be silent in your presence.

—GUIGO II

What if, after we have silenced our world and silenced our soul, we are met not with the soft voice that we expected at last to hear, but with silence?

What if our God is a silent God, who meets our silence with an even greater silence, a silence without beginning or end?

What if silence is not just a condition of our spiritual journey, but its destination; not just a matter of finding ourselves speechless, but accepting that the God we have sought to hear speaks wordlessly?

We were not, if we are honest with ourselves, expecting this: "Won't somebody say something? Won't someone fill the empty space with what makes us comfortable?"

But God speaks not in words, but in presence.

It is said of those who love each other that at some time they achieve the ability to be silent together. They don't need to talk. They share in silence. They may never grow used to it. It may never be their preference. But that's the way it is with lovers.

LET US PRAY

Here in this night,
may I be content with your silence,
and you with mine.

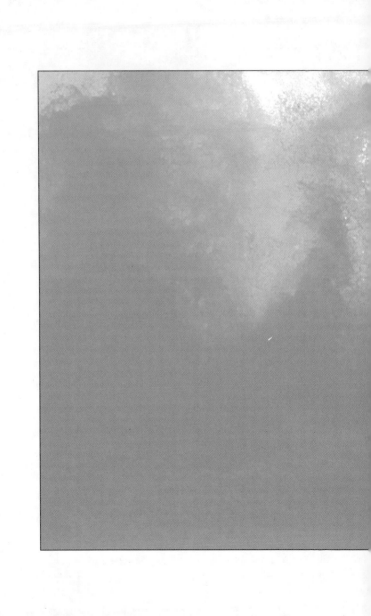

Ignorance

NICHOLAS OF CUSA

You, God,
are all that is desirable
in everything that I desire,
but you remain incomprehensible and infinite.
The more I understand
that I cannot understand you,
the closer I come to what
I have sought to know.
And the more I treasure you
beyond anything and everything
that can be measured and known,
the more I find my rest
in ignorance beyond desire.

—NICHOLAS OF CUSA

Ignorance

To be ignorant, as the dictionary has it, means to be uneducated, unaware, uninformed.

Normally, therefore, we are not given to proclaiming our ignorance. But faced with God, that is precisely what we are called upon to do.

For to be ignorant of the divine is outside the dictionary categories. It is not a failure on our part that might be overcome with additional information, by reading up, by a little bit more effort or a more powerful native intelligence. It is a moment of essential humility, the beginning of spiritual wisdom. It is an admission that there are things—there is One—beyond our knowing.

Normally this fact is described in an abstract language that softens its spiritual impact. "God is the unknown and unknowable, the ultimate mystery." We can live with that.

But to admit to being "ignorant" is to accept and even embrace a word that we have avoided all our lives. It is to embrace plain talk that won't let us off the hook when it comes to our dealing with God. It closes off our exits into spiritual language that lets us pretend that we know something about God that we do not know, that in fact we cannot know.

There is something about this admission that reminds us forcefully that it is not refined language and esoteric knowledge that we bring to God, but raw faith.

As in all other things, in matters of faith our language is turned upside down.

We can't put our trust in any words or images, or any other substitutes for God. We must believe in a God we cannot know, who is unknowable, but who is not unreachable.

Such ignorance has its place, as Nicholas of Cusa well knew. For such ignorance is not a vacuum. It is not the false bliss of "blindered" existence. It is not "nothing." It is its own wisdom. It is the basic condition that we must accept if we are to enter into the world of mystery, for only there can we meet and love God.

It is letting go of our need to know.

Nicholas of Cusa
(1401-1464)

In the history of western spirituality Nicholas of Cusa is the last person you would expect to settle for ignorance.

He was a scholar who was never a specialist but a universal thinker, an intellectual whose insights were wide ranging. He was a lawyer and a historian of law, a mathematician, an astronomer, and a significant figure in the study of scientific method, a mapmaker, a theologian, an ecclesiastical diplomat and a philosopher. And rare for his times, he was a sympathetic student of other religions, especially Islam.

But when it came to speaking of God, the best we can manage, this great intellectual said, is an "informed ignorance"—the name of his most famous work. Concepts won't do. God cannot be shrunk to the size of our mind. His infinitude cannot be captured by our finitude. Only in symbols, the work of our creative imagination, can we somehow touch the infinity of God.

This was a man as unapologetically at home with the most sophisticated intellectual currents of his time as he was with the symbolic life of his soul. There was a place in his mind and soul for "knowledge" and for "learned ignorance." He never felt that he had to choose one or the other. Although God escapes the range of our intellect, he is no less real.

Nicholas' insightful faith is well suited to a time like ours. We are told that something that cannot be measured or weighed does not exist, cannot matter. After all, how do you compare the certitude of an equation with the fleeting mystery of an image?

Nicholas is well suited to a time when we would rather die than say: "I don't know."

After all, who do you know who proclaims their ignorance—as surely we must?

Who willingly lets go of their need to know?

I

Your face cannot be seen except veiled.

—NICHOLAS OF CUSA

Our search for God is not some kind of spiritual game of hide-and-seek.

God does not veil his face to hide from us, to play with our deepest desires, to make us look ridiculous—the butt of some humiliating divine sense of humor that leads us to think that he will be visible just beyond the next turn of an unending maze.

"Sorry. You must have blinked. Better luck next time!"

We have not been tricked into playing peek-a-boo with God because God, in fact, does not veil his face at all.

What seems to us to be a veil covering her face is not a veil, but our own humanity. With limited eyes we cannot see what is without limits. With words that are our creation we cannot describe what is uncreated. With only the light of the world at our disposal we cannot pierce what is for our humanity an impenetrable darkness.

But our blindness is sight. Because of it we cannot mistake God for images of our own creation, cannot forget that it is faith alone that allows us to live beyond the veil.

LET US PRAY

As this day passes into night,
let me embrace its darkness,
all that I cannot see,
all for which I have no words.
Let me treasure you
beyond everything
that I know and see,
and find my rest this night
in letting go of my desire,
and my need to know.

2

. . . That very darkness reveals your face to be there, beyond all veils.

—NICHOLAS OF CUSA

We grow impatient with our humanity, with our blindness, with our inadequate words for what we feel most deeply, what we desire most passionately.

Some sight, we think, would be better than none. Some stumbling words better than finding ourselves speechless, some light better than darkness. Some God, any God, would be better than the faceless God who is visible only to faith.

We are tempted to stop short of the darkness that summons us, tempted to construct a God with a familiar face, a God made in the image and likeness of our finitude.

We are tempted by a God who is available this side of faith.

But an unveiled God, a God who does not require faith, is no God at all but only a construct of our wishful thinking.

It is in the darkness, and only in the darkness, that our God reveals the face that is beyond all the veils woven from our humanity.

It is a face visible only to souls that have become accustomed to the dark.

LET US PRAY

As this day passes into night,
I pray that my fear of the dark
will not tie me to what I can see,
to what I can find words for,
to what I can understand.
Let your darkness
wash over me
and in that darkness
come to me and bless my blindness.
Hear the words I cannot speak.

3

Even unveiled your face is not seen,
until we enter into a certain secret and
mystic silence where there is no knowledge
or concept of face.

—NICHOLAS OF CUSA

Nicholas' secret and mystic silence sounds more exotic, more unattainable than it is. He is simply saying that until we leave behind any notion that we can know and understand God, we will not understand or accept the informed ignorance that lies at the heart of faith.

Such faith will elude us until we enter into and embrace that silence where we can summon up the courage and humility to say: "I don't know because I can't know."

In that same silence we will no longer seek to see what cannot be seen. We will leave behind our temptation to settle for a divine face fashioned to our specifications and enter into a space where the very concept of face is not known.

Nicholas is not putting God beyond our reach. He is in fact closing a distance cluttered with false Gods, clearing our way into that prayerful silence where we need not speak when we have nothing to say, where we wait in silence to be spoken to.

He is leading us into that prayerful silence where we need not put on our best face.

LET US PRAY

As this day passes into night,
silence my soul
and all its desires.
Help me to find my way
into the dark
that lies beyond the clutter of this day
and the sounds of this night.
Help me to put aside
if just for this moment
my clumsy attempts
at trying to understand what cannot be understood.
And for this moment be content
with the darkness.

4

In all faces
is seen the Face of faces.

—NICHOLAS OF CUSA

Here is the mystery and the irony: The face that cannot be seen is visible wherever we look.

In all faces is seen the Face of the unseen. In all voices is heard the Voice of the voiceless.

But it takes faith to penetrate the veil of our own blindness to glimpse the features of God in the face of our neighbor and to hear her voice whenever and wherever the voiceless struggle exists.

We see the unseeable God when we see each other. We hear the silence of God when we hear each other. But we miss the face of God when we look without seeing, and we miss her voice when we listen without hearing.

"When did I see you hungry and did not feed you?"

"When did I see you naked and did not clothe you?"

"When did I see you homeless and did not shelter you?"

"Look again. It is my face in the faces you see."

LET US PRAY

As this day passes into night,
silence my soul until I can hear
the voices
that I was deaf to this day.
When did you call out to me?
When did I see you?
Here in the dark
let me see the faces that I passed by.
let me see in them
your face.
Let me hear in their voices
your voice.

5

We may always praise God for showing Godself to us as incomprehensible.

—NICHOLAS OF CUSA

"Truth," Nicholas wrote, "shines forth incomprehensibly in the darkness of our ignorance."

"That may be true," we find ourselves replying, "but it can seem like playing word games when what we hunger for is a sight of God."

Nicholas answers that "God is known to God alone." We should therefore "praise God for showing himself as incomprehensible."

It cannot be otherwise. To seek a comprehensible God is to seek less than God. It is to put our God-hungry souls on a starvation diet.

It is to deny to ourselves the kind of knowing that is available only to faith, to the light that "shines forth incomprehensibly in the darkness of our ignorance. "

These are not word games. Not spiritual double-speak. Ignorance is our spiritual homeland. Know-it-alls are out of place.

Faith is our only passport.

LET US PRAY

As this day passes into night,
remind my soul
that you shine brightest,
that your presence is most deeply felt
when I surrender to the darkness of the night,
when I admit to my ignorance.
Let me go
where only faith can take me.
Let night and your darkness
bring light to my soul.

Faith

KARL RAHNER

The ultimate conviction and decision of faith
comes in the last resort,
not from a pedagogic indoctrination from
outside,
supported by public opinion in secular society
or in the church,
nor from a merely rational argumentation of
fundamental theology,
but from the experience of God,
of his spirit,
of his freedom,
bursting out of the very heart of human existence
and able to be really experienced there,
even though this experience cannot be wholly
a matter for reflection
or be verbally objectified.

—KARL RAHNER

Faith

Faith and its spiritual expressions only appear to be abstractions, changeless states of our mind and soul. Karl Rahner knew differently. He knew that they are always lived out in a specific time and place.

He foresaw, for example, that faith in the future would not be just "more of the same." There was a time when faith was supported by a sociological homogeneity. Everybody in the county was Irish or German. Whole countries shared a common religious faith. Support was in the air they breathed. We practiced not just the faith of our fathers, but of our next door neighbor and everybody else in town. Not any more. The extraordinary support system of a shared belief, of a shared religious experience, of a shared religious language is a luxury that is no longer ours.

The conclusion he reached, however, was not to whine about the change or try to reconstruct a no longer possible world, but to strike at the very heart of faithful living in our times.

In the future, he wrote—read "now"—our spirituality "will have to be lived much more clearly than hitherto, out of a solitary, immediate experience of God and his spirit in the individual."

Read on:

"In such a situation the lonely responsibility of the individual in his or her decision of faith is necessary and required in a way much more radical than it was in former times."

He is proclaiming a time of radical faith. We have to shape our spirituality in an "historical situation imposed on us and not made by us."

The act of faith has always involved personal responsibility. It has never been something we could shift to someone else—an individual or a whole community. Living faith has always required much more than joining the club or living in religious synch with our neighbors.

But history has made mysticism imperative.

Ready or not, we believers must be mystics or "we will not exist at all—if by mysticism we mean, not singular parapsychological phenomena, but a genuine experience of God emerging from the very heart of our existence."

Karl Rahner
(1904-1984)

In our day world class theologians are not expected to write essays about devotion to the Sacred Heart of Jesus. That sort of thing is considered more appropriate to unenlightened preachers and our grandmother's prayer books. Theologians, it seems, are expected to look down upon such expressions of faith as pious sentimentality.

Enter Karl Rahner.

Without question one of the most respected, inventive, and influential theologians of the twentieth century, he is someone who recognizes the simple heart of the most profound mystic, and the profound heart of our most commonplace experiences. He has, without condescension or apologies, written essays on popular piety that take an honored place in a canon of more than three thousand publications that often tax the intellectual limits of the brightest students. He has no time for those who write and act as though they have a lock on God. He warns them—and us—of burying our experience of God under layers of "theological, ascetic and pious chatter." His writings on spirituality are almost as numerous as his scientific papers. There is no question that his conviction that the most scholarly theology and the most practical spirituality belong together runs through his life and work.

There were others things that he saw as belonging together. Ordained as a Jesuit priest into a theological universe that had become increasingly static and confining, he developed over the years a style of theology that brought together the reigning Thomism with existentialist and transcendental philosophy. He was at home with Kant, Heidegger, and Husserl. He was also at home with world religions and saw grace at work in them. He saw the inevitability of change in a church that boasted of its changeless character. And he knew that Christianity would have to shed its European trappings and prejudices and become a world citizen.

But it is what he brought together in his own life that was at the heart of his broad acceptance and recognition. Karl Lehman and Albert Raffert, two of his most perceptive and devoted students and editors, put it this way: "in him we find a deep and simple faith, penetrated alike with a rare passion for the incomprehensible God and a subdued (but all the more genuine for it) human intimacy and goodness."

I

God himself and nothing else is our eternal life.

—KARL RAHNER

"I'll tell you what would make me happy, your role is to help me get it."

No one of us would admit to a prayer of such brazen self-interest—and attempted divine manipulation—but a few minutes reflection might shock us by revealing how close this description comes to our reality.

All of us treasure a notion of what could make us happy and almost without exception it falls far short of final and complete surrender to a hidden God. We prefer happiness that is within our power to imagine and define. Something we can wrap our hopes around, something within our grasp. Instead we are offered a happiness that is incomprehensible, mysterious, and hidden.

"God and nothing else is our eternal life."

What we overlook in our search for substitutes is that this hidden God is not inaccessible but immediately available to us in every passing moment. The incomprehensible, the mysterious, and the hidden are the inner reality of everything we see and touch.

Our task is to dig ourselves out from under the layers that we have so steadily used to cover up the God who is there, who has been there since first we breathed.

LET US PRAY

As this night begins,
I reach out to you
incomprehensible,
mysterious,
and hidden
in the darkness,
inseparable from the night
in which we meet.
But I am not mistaken,
I know that it is you to whom I surrender
here in the night.

2

God, who is our absolute future,
is the incomprehensible mystery.

—KARL RAHNER

Because our spiritual journey is not a theological exercise, it does not reward us with increasing clarity. Rather it submerges us ever more deeply in mystery.

So as long as we see God as our future, the depth of our surrender to what is beyond our comprehension will be the measure of our life. Mystery will be the air we breathe, incomprehensible mystery our destined and chosen future.

Faith will be our way of life.

It is not an easy path to walk. We like to *see* where we are going. More to the point, we like to *know* where we are going. And, it seems we forever want to know whether we are there yet, and more importantly, if there is any "there" there.

Our future, however, is not in knowing.

It is not *in* God or *about* God.

Our future is an incomprehensible mystery. It is God.

LET US PRAY

As this night begins
I am more aware than ever
that I cannot *see* where I am going.
More to the point
I don't even *know*
where I am going.
Only this:
with every step,
with every prayer,
I go further into the dark,
further into the mystery
that you are.

3

God desires to be the ultimate happiness of
man, in his incomprehensibility
and not despite it.

—KARL RAHNER

And Rahner adds: "this is the key to man's own self-understanding."

Our ultimate happiness lies not in understanding God or inventing an understandable God, but in resting our hope of such happiness in the fact that God cannot be understood.

An understandable God could never offer us ultimate happiness, because the other side of this coin is that in accepting the incomprehensibility of God as our ultimate happiness, we become aware that our happiness depends equally as much on discovering and accepting our own incomprehensibility.

Our self-understanding can go only so far, reach only so deep. We understand that beyond our understanding, our search for happiness is a tale of mystery confronting and confronted by mystery. At that moment when we accept our own mysterious being, our life begins, our hopes take root, we can accept that it is in mystery and not despite it that we will find our happiness.

Mystery is where we come to life, where we come to live.

We are a mystery in search of mystery.

LET US PRAY

As this night begins,
I want nothing more than
to bring with me into its darkness
my own darkness,
my own mystery,
for here is where
I come to life
where I have always been
meant to live.
It is precisely the darkness of the night
that assures me that I am
where I should be.

4

The perfect beatitude granted to man by
God consists in immediate access to God.

—KARL RAHNER

There are in our lives certain quiet, prayerful moments when we let ourselves dream of experiencing God, of having immediate access to her presence. But to be honest, most of the time we don't really expect that to happen. We are prepared—even in our quietest, most hopeful moments—to settle for less, for far less.

We are prepared to live out our days as bit players, content to mumble our prayers and hope for the best.

We accept that we are not in the same league with the mystics whose words we have come not only to rely on even though the pattern of their lives seems so different from the ordinariness of our days.

We find it hard, even impossible to think of ourselves as mystics. The idea seems to us to be sheer spiritual pretentiousness.

That's when we need to hear Rahner clearly: the believer "of the future will be a mystic or he or she will not exist at all—if by mysticism we mean, not singular parapsychological phenomena, but a genuine experience of God emerging from the very heart of our existence."

He is talking about us. About our heart. About our existence. About our essential mystery.

LET US PRAY

Here in the night,
help me to accept
that experiencing you
is meant to be the commonplace
center of my life.
Help me to hear you clearly,
however darkly
when you talk to me
about my heart,
about my existence,
about my essential mystery.

5

Allow basic, ultimate human experiences to come first.

—KARL RAHNER

We can't say it or hear it too often: "the experience of God is not something rare and exotic."

It is primitive, even raw, and it can, in the startling language of Rahner, seem "banal." God emerges from the depths of our soul when we choose not to escape but to take seriously the commonplace, everyday, bare facts of our humanity and their mysterious core.

God is present and accessible when we "face loneliness, fear, and imminent death." But he is just as accessible in our far more ordinary "longing for truth, for love, for fellowship, for God."

It is left to us to recognize these experiences for what they are so that "something like a primitive awareness of God can emerge."

But it is also for us to understand that for all its primitive strength and energy it is an awareness that is easily buried under the routine of our day and by, as Rahner says, our " theological, ascetic and pious chatter."

Digging, to keep uncovered our primitive, mystery embedded roots will be the task of our lifetime.

LET US PRAY

As this night begins,
remind me yet again
that you are not absent,
just covered over
by the layers of this
and all the other days,
especially by the words
that I have erected
like a wall
to protect my heart
against your simple strength.
Quiet the chatter.
If just for tonight.

PART THREE

Unbelief

In all faces
is seen the Face of faces,
veiled, enigmatic;
even unveiled it is not seen,
until above all faces
we enter into a certain secret
and mystic silence
where there is no knowledge or
concept of face.
Your face cannot be seen except veiled;
but that very darkness
reveals your face to be there,
beyond all veils.

—NICHOLAS OF CUSA

No matter how good it is to be in their company spending time with spiritual superstars can leave the rest of us feeling like non-starters.

For the most part we don't have dramatic dark nights of the soul. We have headachy mornings when it takes all the believing we can muster to put breakfast on the table, lunch in a bag, kids on a school bus, and a positive face on a work place that is draining what patience, energy and self-respect we have left. On the other hand we are seldom caught up in spiritual raptures that transform our dull days into ecstatic adventures. Of course neither were the saints.

Maybe there should be a shrine to the unknown believer where those of us who are exasperatingly ordinary could gather to exchange war stories and plant a wreath. No perfect souls, no superstars need apply because perfection is not a standard that seems applicable or appropriate to our oh-too-human lives, and the dailiness of our oh-too-human faith.

But nothing proves to be a greater stumbling block than our own expectations. Perfection is precisely the impossible standard to which many of us were educated and to which part of our soul still clings. Our goal was to be faultless. Held out in many programs of spirituality was the practice of examining our conscience daily—it was called the *particular examen*. The carrot being offered was that even a slow believer could wipe out a fault every week or so. At this rate perfection was just months away, certainly no more than a year or two. Of course it never happened. It couldn't. The expectations of such an education overlooked our humanity.

We are not God. Nor are we supposed to become God whose nature it is to be perfect. We are by nature imperfect. The best we can hope for is to be perfectly human.

What applied to the pursuit of virtue applies in spades to believing.

Everything that is received, the old philosophers used to say, is received in the mode of the receiver. Human faith cannot exist in any way other than in the mode of our humanity—that is, in the mode of limitation and finitude. So in the long run every story of perfect human faith sought turns out to be a tale marbled through with questioning, hesitation, doubt, and unbelief. It is just the way it is, just the way we are. Faith will always be imperfect. It will always mirror the limitations, the finitude of our humanity.

It will also always mock our need for and our expectation of the kind of mathematical certitude we were taught to expect from the world around us.

We were told what was sacred and what was human, what was right and what was wrong. We had a picture-perfect image of the world. Our life task would be mostly to live within the boundaries that our certitudes marked out. We came to know and live in a world where two and two always makes four.

And we came to expect that our relationship to God would fit into that world. We hoped that it would. But it can't. And it wouldn't.

The world in which we relate to God as adults can never enjoy the certitude of childhood religion. Adult faith is about mystery. It doesn't have to do with facts or with creeds. It is a relationship. It is not captive to equations but begins and ends in what is not just unknown but unknowable. There are no equal signs when we talk about God.

Adult faith, therefore, is not a synonym for some higher certitude or some substitute security. It is our way of living with mystery. It is a way of knowing God, ourselves and our world that plants its roots in the unknowable. It is the way we live when we are convinced that what is important to us is beyond our knowing.

It demands of us that we cross over from the certitude of childhood religion to the ambiguities of adult faith, that we accept that we can no longer borrow and live on the certitudes of our family, our community, our church, our teachers, and our guardians. Nor can we rely on their faith.

It is in such a moment that a faith-rooted adult spiritual life can begin.

**

We have, too often, another expectation that becomes a stumbling block.

We expect to experience God's presence as a reward for our faith.

It doesn't happen that way.

God's presence remains a veiled presence, an unending demand for faith. For whether sensed or missed, God's presence is accessible only by our willingness to suspend our dependence on what can be seen and surrender ourselves to what is forever beyond our sight, our willingness to entrust our lives to a veiled God.

This doesn't mean that our desire to see God face to face will go away, or that our desire to pull back the curtain and raise the veil will disappear. We will go on harboring the hope that the veil hiding God is a kind of scrim. At any moment, we hope, the lights behind it will go on and reveal the presence beyond the veil, the face we have only imagined.

It won't happen because behind every veil there is a veil, seventy thousand veils as the wise Sufis have it.

Still it is much easier to talk of veils than to accept their reality.

We want to see God. We hunger for God's presence. It is not easy to be told that we will have to wait indefinitely, that short of the grave there is nothing to look forward to but a veiled presence, a veiled absence.

Surely if we pray as we should, if we leave our heart open, our reward will be a glimpse of the God for whom we so hunger. And surely God's protracted absence is because we have not prayed well enough, because we have closed our heart to God's advances.

But God is no closer, no more loving on days when the veil is transparent than on the days when it yields only darkness.

Both require faith.

Therese of Lisieux served and loved a God who persisted in remaining hidden behind veils impenetrable to anything but a faith as unfazable as hers. "You might think," she wrote, "that I am a child for whom the veil of faith is almost rent asunder. But it is not a veil. It is a wall which reaches to the very heavens, shutting out the starry skies."

Some days—for some people—that veil is almost transparent, the rough outline of God's features almost visible, God's presence almost tangible.

These are the days that tradition has come to call times of consolation.

For others—on other days—the veil is impenetrable. There is only darkness, emptiness. No one, it seems, is there. The veil hides nothingness.

These are arid times, desert days.

But the veiled face of God is not a sometime thing.

It will remain veiled as long as God is God and as long as we are human.

We will have to live "believing."

A Canadian reviewer of books about Thomas Merton got it about right. Spirituality in our times, he concluded, is destined to be a spirituality of incompleteness and contradiction. We will almost certainly live out our lives without ever experiencing a sense of having it "all together."

"Incompleteness and contradiction—never having it all together" may not be phrases that appear in classical spiritual writing, but they do not belong just to the post-modern age. They belong to the nature of God and the nature of faith.

Some things don't change with the times.

**

Twenty years after the snowy night in the New Jersey mountains I would stand just a few hundred miles south on the edge of the Atlantic watching a storm at sea work its way inland. It was noisy and dramatic. I watched its lightning set dry old telephone poles afire. I saw its waves get higher, stronger. I heard them get louder and closer.

But it was all muffled sound, all gauzy stage setting.

An hour or so earlier in the room at my back I had faced a dozen young men just a step away from ordination to the priesthood. "I hope," a young man said, "that you don't plan to talk about faith. That's your question, not ours. We believe."

"How nice for you," I might have said. "How 'young' of you," I might have said. "How sad for you," I might have said.

What I actually said has long since been forgotten. I probably just nodded some kind of assent.

But an hour later standing at the edge of the storm a nodded assent was not enough. "Those young men say they believe. You have no reason not to take their word. But how about you? Do you believe? Well: do you?"

"I still believe," I might have said, I might have prayed. "But help my unbelief."

That's what I still answer whenever, at the edge of the storm, I hear the question again.

That's what I still answer whenever I am required to walk on water.